FREE

Neil T. Anderson
and Dave Park

Regal

From Gospel Light
Ventura, California, U.S.A.

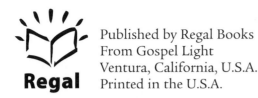

Published by Regal Books
From Gospel Light
Ventura, California, U.S.A.
Printed in the U.S.A.

Gospel Light is a Christian publisher dedicated to serving the local church. We believe God's vision for Gospel Light is to provide church leaders with biblical, user-friendly materials that will help them evangelize, disciple and minister to children, youth and families.

It is our prayer that this Gospel Light resource will help you discover biblical truth for your own life and help you minister to youth. May God richly bless you.

For a free catalog of resources from Gospel Light, please contact your Christian supplier or contact us at 1-800-4-GOSPEL *or* www.gospellight.com.

ISBN 0-8307-3696-4
© Neil T. Anderson and Dave Park
All rights reserved.
Printed in the U.S.A.

Edited by Alex Field

Library of Congress Cataloging-in-Publication Data
Anderson, Neil T., 1942-
   Free : connecting with Jesus, the source of true freedom / Neil T. Anderson and Dave Park.
      p. cm.
   Includes bibliographical references.
   ISBN 0-8307-3696-4 (trade pbk.)
   1. Salvation. 2. Liberty—Religious aspects—Christianity. 3. Jesus Christ. I. Park, David, 1961- II. Title.
   BT751.3.A53 2005
   234—dc22   2005003029

1   2   3   4   5   6   7   8   9   10   /   10   09   08   07   06   05

Rights for publishing this book in other languages are contracted by Gospel Light Worldwide, the international nonprofit ministry of Gospel Light. Gospel Light Worldwide also provides publishing and technical assistance to international publishers dedicated to producing Sunday School and Vacation Bible School curricula and books in the languages of the world. For additional information, visit www.gospellightworldwide.org; write to Gospel Light Worldwide, P.O. Box 3875, Ventura, CA 93006; or send an e-mail to info@gospellightworldwide.org.

DEDICATION

This book is dedicated to the memory of Dan Roeloff, a man who found that place called surrender.

C O N T E N T S

D A Y

ACKNOWLEDGMENTS

We would like to thank Bill Greig III, Bill Denzel, Alex Field, Jessie Minassian, Patti Virtue and Pam Wiebe at Gospel Light. Thank you for sharing our vision to help today's youth discover who they are in Christ and find their freedom in Him!

THE 24/7 CHALLENGE

24/7 means to live for Jesus 24 hours a day, 7 days a week. In other words—all the time! Living for Jesus in this sin-twisted world is tough, but we can do it! God has a special challenge for us, a 24/7 challenge. *Free* is about living our lives for Jesus. God made it possible through His Son for sinners to become saints. That's quite a change. The theological term for this incredible change is "sanctification." We are completely forgiven for every sin we have ever committed or will ever commit, but we have not been perfected. Paul says, "We proclaim him, admonishing and teaching everyone with all wisdom, so that we may present everyone perfect in Christ. To this end I labor, struggling with all his energy, which so powerfully works in me" (Colossians 1:28-29).

Are you ready for a 40-day journey that will help you become more like Jesus and live totally for Him? This adventure takes a small commitment on your part—about 10 minutes a day for the next 40 days. It takes about 40 days to develop a habit, so we want to encourage you to take the challenge to live for Jesus 24/7 by first giving Him 10 minutes of your day. Will you accept the challenge?

I know that without Christ I can do nothing, yet with Him I can do all things. I, _____ [your name], accept the 24/7 challenge to live for Jesus and experience life with Him. I choose to develop, through the leading of the Holy Spirit, a daily time to meet with God and spend time in His awesome presence. I will not fail because His grace has me covered and I'm totally acceptable to Him. I desire to hear His voice and to know and do His will 24/7.

_____

Signature   Date

H O W T O U S E T H I S B O O K

1. Pray against any distractions. Tell Satan, the enemy, to leave you alone. Ask God for understanding and guidance as you set out on this journey.
2. Take your time. Don't hurry to finish the day's insights. Listen to God's voice and try to spot the key verses used each day. Look them up in your Bible to catch the context.
3. Write out your feelings, personal comments and discoveries. By writing down your insights, you will remember what God is teaching you.
4. Answer each of the discussion questions from your own perspective—as they relate to your own personal needs and life.
5. State out loud "The Lie to Reject" and "The Truth to Accept" as well as other statements as recommended.
6. Monitor your progress and keep on track. If you miss a day, make a plan to catch up.
7. Find a quiet place and a special time to meet with God daily. Make sure there are no interruptions or distractions to bug you (like the TV or radio). Even if you are used to studying with the radio on, turn it off for your devotional time so that you can hear God's voice. Find someone who will go through the devotional at the same time you do. Encourage each other and check in to make sure that you are both keeping up.

My accountability partner is _____.

Y O U C A N D O I T !

Our prayer is that this book will help you live like the person you really are in Jesus. You have a new identity and a personal guide—Jesus—to help you become more like Him, so you can do it! We also hope this book opens up many ministry opportunities for you to share these truths with others. We know God will bless your time with Him!

The Search

God sacrificed Jesus on the altar of the world to clear that world of sin. Having faith in him sets us in the clear. God decided on this course of action in full view of the public—to set the world in the clear with himself through the sacrifice of Jesus, finally taking care of the sins he had so patiently endured. This is not only clear, but it's now—this is current history! God sets things right. He also makes it possible for us to live in his rightness.

Romans 3:21-22, *THE MESSAGE*

Here's an old story from the 1800s:

> There came down one of the rough mountain roads of Mexico a
> few years ago a weary-looking, travel-stained man. As he walked
> along he examined every landmark on the way, and at last seemed
> to find the place he was looking for. It was a rough, uncultivated,
> hilly piece of land not much good for growing anything, but this
> did not appear to disappoint the traveler. On the contrary, he
> hurried to find out from the owners if the land could be bought
> and soon had obtained it for hardly anything. Then day after day,
> the Mexican man patiently toiled with plough, spade and pick,
> but (as he sowed no seed) for what reason no one knew. Months
> rolled away, and as means and strength began to fail, the man
> found two others to help in his work. To them he told a secret
> that made them toil as patiently and persistently as himself.
>
> A dying man had confessed to him that a few years ago he
> had belonged to a band of robbers that had fallen upon and
> destroyed a troop of soldiers. The poor fellows were convoying
> over the mountains an immense quantity of silver dollars. And
> in defending their charge, they were all killed. When the slaugh-
> ter was over, the robbers had been bitterly disappointed to find
> that during the fight the treasure had disappeared. They were
> certain that it was concealed, but in spite of a most diligent
> search they had to leave without it. Most of them were very
> shortly afterward surrounded and killed. The incident had
> almost been forgotten. The dying robber had described the scene
> of the encounter with the soldiers, and the one to whom he had
> confided the secret was now seeking the lost treasure.
>
> Seven long years passed and still the search was being carried
> on. At last there came a day when, worn out with toil, the owner
> of the land lay at death's door. Away among the hills his com-
> rades were hard at work dislodging a great rock. And when they
> had succeeded there appeared to their eager eyes the entrance to
> a cave. At once the treasure seekers rushed in feeling sure that all
> of their labor was to be rewarded. But not a single dollar was to

be found. The men were turning to leave the cave when they caught sight of an old piece of leather hanging from a dark cleft in the rock above. They gave it a pull and it came down in their hands—and with it came rolling down at their feet a few silver dollars for which they had so long searched in vain. Soon the whole treasure was discovered and the finders were rich men. The leather bags that contained the money had been hastily cast in some hole above and were quickly covered with stones and earth, thus escaping the searchers' eyes.

Heaps of the silver dollars were carried into the hut where the sick man lay. He saw and handled them. But they profited him nothing. For either on the same day or the following day he died. The years of toil had only brought him weariness, broken health and death.[1]

The old man spent his life in a vain search for silver. It sounds ridiculous, doesn't it? No one would be so stupid as to spend his or her entire life in search of earthly wealth. Oh, really? We see that vain search going on all around us. People are spending their lives in the relentless pursuit of a little more. Jesus talked about a greater search and a real life in Matthew 16. He said:

> If anyone wishes to come after Me, he must deny himself, and take up his cross and follow Me. For whoever wishes to save his life will lose it; but whoever loses his life for My sake will find it. For what will it profit a man if he gains the whole world and forfeits his soul? Or what will a man give in exchange for his soul? For the Son of Man is going to come in the glory of His Father with His angels, and will then repay every man according to his deeds (Matthew 16:24-27, *NASB*).

Have you ever wished you had complete control of your life? Have you ever wished that no one could tell you what to do? Have you ever wished that you had no curfews set by your parents or no tardy slips given out at school?

Sometimes we think that when we get out of school or move out of our parents' home, we'll be in charge of our own lives. But that just isn't true. The Bible shoots straight with us. It says we'll either be slaves to God or slaves to sin and Satan. Jesus said, "Everyone who sins is a slave to sin" (John 8:34). The Bible makes it clear that when we're serving our own selfish ambitions, we aren't serving God. Anytime we aren't serving God, we're really serving Satan. Romans 6:11-13 (*NASB*) goes on to tell us:

> Even so consider yourselves to be dead to sin, but alive to God in Christ Jesus. Therefore do not let sin reign in your mortal body so that you obey its lusts, and do not go on presenting the members of your body to sin as instruments of unrighteousness; but present yourselves to God as those alive from the dead, and your members as instruments of righteousness to God.

Some would say, "I am just going along with what everyone else is doing." But these verses are telling us that if we live like those in the world around us, it is the same as our being slaves to sin and Satan. The good news is that we don't have to be slaves to sin. We can be free because of what Christ did for us and we can choose to live a new life of godliness in which we seek to serve God and do His will (see John 12:24-26). Some mornings we may not feel very holy, but we don't live according to our feelings. We look to God's truth that, unlike our feelings, doesn't change. So when we wake up, we would do well to remind ourselves that all of our sins have been taken away and forgiven through Christ's loving work on the Cross. "When you were stuck in your old sin-dead life, you were incapable of responding to God. God brought you alive—right along with Christ! Think of it! All sins forgiven, the slate wiped clean, that old arrest warrant canceled and nailed to Christ's Cross" (Colossians 2:13-14, *THE MESSAGE*).

Even though Christ died for our sins and we are completely forgiven, that doesn't mean the battle is over. We need the Holy Spirit's help because we have a job to do. We need to make the choice to turn away from the world, the flesh and the enemy's call, and listen to the Word and voice of God. If we listen to the world, we'll live like the world. If we listen to God and heed His Word, we'll be able to follow Jesus and experience the joy of real fellowship with Him. The decision to live for Jesus isn't controlled by the world, our flesh or any fallen spirit. It's ours alone. Not even our parents, friends or youth pastors can make that decision for us.

As you read those words, were you thinking, *I want to live for Jesus. I want to follow Him with all my heart. I just don't seem to have the power to live that way.* Where does the power to live for Jesus come from? The ability to follow Jesus comes from the Holy Spirit who lives inside you. If the Spirit isn't leading you, you'll soon get tired of resisting temptation and give in to sin. But if the Spirit leads you, you will do the will of God.

How we identified ourselves before we knew Jesus as a personal Savior no longer applies to us after we put our trust in Him. When we look back to our B.C. days ("B.C." stands for "before Christ"), we might recall dozens of sinful and evil things that we did. But it doesn't do us any good to reflect on those old sinful days, unless we also recall how Jesus saved us. Yes, we were sinful. And we would do well not to forget how empty, painful and meaningless life was without Christ. But God wants us to move on and realize that we have been changed because of what He has done for us. We need to understand who we are now that Christ has died for us and forgiven us. We don't want to get our identity from who we were before we knew Christ but rather see ourselves as Christ sees us. Because of Christ, we are holy. Our identity doesn't come from doing holy things, however. We have been made holy through Christ's death, burial and resurrection.

Now that you know Christ, you've been transformed from a sinner into a child of God—a saint. You are one of God's divine masterpieces. Right now He is putting all of His finishing touches on you so that someday you will be just like Jesus. You are no longer a product of your past and your sinful failures. You are now one of Jesus' great works of art, being hand-tooled by the Master Himself. The question is, Do you want to identify with your work in your life and your old sinful ways before you knew Christ, or do you want to identify with Jesus' work in your life? Growing up to be like Jesus isn't easy. But it will be even harder if you see yourself in light of your past rather than in light of who you are in Christ. The truth is that you've been changed and are free to grow in God's grace and be all that He has called you to be.

In the opening story, the old man traveled a rough road to find lost treasure. He dug and toiled for years with nothing to show for it. He never got to spend a dime of the hidden silver he had looked for. It's so different for those of us who follow Jesus! We are not on a journey to find silver and gold. We are on the trail of true treasure—the victorious Christian life and the peace that comes from following Jesus. We are rewarded every day as we follow Jesus and experience His presence.

How serious are you about living for Jesus? Would you sell out Jesus if someone gave you a million dollars? Would you give up His leading or hearing His voice for silver? Would you trade the treasures that last forever for a single reward today? I don't think so! Walking with Jesus offers a freedom, a peace and a joy that nothing else can give. You can have all the money in the world, but it still won't buy you peace. You can experience all of Earth's pleasures and still feel empty inside and have no joy. Only when you know who you are in Christ will you experience the abundant life He has prepared for you and experience real life.

Discussion

- People spend their lives in the relentless pursuit of more—more money, more possessions, more power. How are you spending your time? What is really important to you?
- What three things did Jesus ask us to do in Matthew 16:24?
- We are not our own masters. The Bible tells us that we are either slaves to God or slaves to what?
- Our true identity lies in the fact that we are now what?

The Lie to Reject

I reject the lie that my life is my own to control or to live for selfish reasons.

The Truth to Accept

I announce the truth that I am called to live for Jesus 24 hours a day, 7 days a week—24/7.

Prayer

Dear heavenly Father, You challenge me to deny myself, to take up my cross and to follow You. Lord, I desire to do just that! I know that I wouldn't profit by gaining the whole world and losing my soul. Instead, I choose to live for You! I want to make my life count—to live a real life in Jesus. In Jesus' name I pray. Amen.

Reading

1 Corinthians 1

Stay Balanced!

Let the peace of Christ rule in your hearts, to which indeed
you were called in one body; and be thankful. Let the word of
Christ richly dwell within you, with all wisdom teaching and
admonishing one another with psalms and hymns and spiritual
songs, singing with thankfulness in your hearts to God.
Colossians 3:15-16, *NASB*

If you know anything about football, you have heard of Vince Lombardi. A story has circulated about his last season as head coach of the Green Bay Packers.

On this day, Vince Lombardi faced a difficult challenge: Where to begin after yesterday's humiliating defeat. There was little he could say to his team that hadn't already been said. There were few aspects of the game that they had not practiced and analyzed extensively. The men were professionals. They knew their performance on the field had been atrocious. They were angry, frustrated, and disappointed—to say the least.

In his remarkable manner, Lombardi met the challenge head-on. Picking up the familiar, leather ball, he went directly to the heart of the matter. In a deliberate manner he brought everyone's attention back to the basics with five simple words: "Men, this is a football." One of his players who understood exactly how badly they needed to review the essentials spoke up, "Hold on, Coach, you're going too fast!"[2]

Every Christian knows something about salvation, yet many are easily confused about the concepts of salvation and sanctification since both are presented in the Bible in the past, present and future verb tenses. Like Lombardi's Green Bay Packers, we need to go back to the basics. Let's start by taking a look at what the Bible says as it relates to our salvation.

Because of His great love for us, God, who is rich in mercy, made us alive with Christ even when we were dead in transgressions— it is by grace you have been saved. For it is by grace you have been saved, through faith—and this not from yourselves, it is the gift of God (Ephesians 2:4-5,8).

Join with me in suffering for the gospel, by the power of God, who has saved us and called us to a holy life—not because of anything we have done but because of his own purpose and grace (2 Timothy 1:8-9).

When the kindness and love of God our Savior appeared, he saved us, not because of righteous things we had done, but because of his mercy. He saved us through the washing of rebirth and renewal by the Holy Spirit (Titus 3:4-5).

According to those verses, the Bible clearly teaches that all of us who have put our trust in Christ have experienced salvation. We are children of God, and we've been made spiritually alive. Jesus said, "I am the resurrection and the life. He who believes in me will live, even though he dies; and whoever lives and believes in me will never die" (John 11:25-26).

Because we put our trust in Christ, we've been made spiritually alive. Our soul and spirit will stay alive even when our physical body dies. Because of our belief in Christ, we will never die spiritually. But hold on to your hat, there's more! The Bible also tells us we are *presently* being saved. Check out these verses:

The message of the cross is foolishness to those who are perishing, but to us who are being saved it is the power of God (1 Corinthians 1:18).

We are to God the aroma of Christ among those who are being saved and those who are perishing (2 Corinthians 2:15).

My dear friends, as you have always obeyed—not only in my presence, but now much more in my absence—continue to work out your salvation with fear and trembling (Philippians 2:12).

When you read those passages, you might walk away thinking, *So, I have to do good works for my salvation.* Hold on! We don't want you to make that mistake. That is not what these verses say. We do not work *for* our salvation, but we are called to work *out* what God has started in us. Did you catch the difference? When you think of salvation, you will always need to remember God's holiness. Apart from the gift of Jesus, we as human beings are not holy. We don't do good works of holiness to attain our salvation. Rather, we receive salvation and God's holiness as a free gift. Now that we've been made holy, true salvation will show itself in our lives.

We were saved the moment we accepted Christ, and when we die we are going to heaven. But salvation is still at work in our lives, conforming us to the image of God. Even though our salvation begins on Earth, it is completed in heaven.

That is why the Bible speaks about a future aspect of salvation. Check out these verses, which teach we "shall be saved":

Since we have now been justified by his blood, how much more shall we be saved from God's wrath through him (Romans 5:9)!

The hour has come for you to wake up from your slumber, because our salvation is nearer now than when we first believed (Romans 13:11).

Christ was sacrificed once to take away the sins of many people; and he will appear a second time, not to bear sin, but to bring salvation to those who are waiting for him (Hebrews 9:28).

We like to think of salvation as it relates to a single point in time—that moment when we prayed to receive Christ. It's good to recognize the specific time when each of us accepted Christ, but salvation doesn't just touch our lives for a mere moment. For instance, we have not yet been saved from the wrath that is to come, but we have the assurance that we will be. "Having believed, you were marked in him with a seal, the promised Holy Spirit, who is a deposit guaranteeing our inheritance until the redemption of those who are God's possession—to the praise of his glory" (Ephesians 1:13-14).

When the Bible talks about salvation and sanctification, we need to understand that both of these biblical truths are at work from the moment we first receive Christ until we die and are finally made perfect like Jesus. Salvation and sanctification are at work from our new birth all the way to our glorification.

Have you ever been to a circus? Any good circus has a tightrope walker. The cheap, wimpy circuses just have a single tightrope walker. But the good ones have layers of people. Some tightrope walkers walk across the rope, two at a time, with a thin pole on their shoulders. In the center of the pole a third person sits, balancing on a chair. Think of the balance and timing it would take to keep all three from falling. Each person on the wire has to make delicate adjustments to stay in sync with the others.

In the same way, if we want to live a stable Christian life, we need to find the biblical balance between what God does for us (His sovereignty) and our own personal responsibility. Both are clearly taught in Bible.

Picture yourself sitting in the chair between the two tightrope walkers. The one in front is our view of God's sovereignty. The one behind you is your view of your personal responsibility. If one view gets out of balance, you will take a fall.

Similarly, the process of becoming like Jesus (sanctification) requires some delicate maneuvering. It is easy to see how we can lose our balance one way or the other if we look at the two extreme views of sanctification. Picking either extreme will mess up the process of being conformed to the image of God. That's why balance is so important.

If we emphasize the past tense or positional aspects of sanctification and overlook the ongoing need to live out our holiness, we will fall off the rope. If we claim holiness and overlook the reality of sin in our own personal lives and the necessity to assume responsibility for our growth, we will fall off the rope. This can lead to a denial of our own faults, and we'll end up having to pretend that we have it all together when we don't.

On the other hand, if we emphasize the progressive aspects of sanctification we'll think that we'll never be holy until we die. This wrong view overlooks all the references to the past-tense realities of sanctification.

I hope you are asking, "How can I be balanced?" The answer to that question is found in humility. To sit in that center chair requires a humble balance because at either extreme is pride. Leaning toward the first tightrope walker are those who think more highly of themselves than they ought (see Romans 12:3). They say, "We're already holy in Christ. We don't need to concern ourselves with sin or growing toward holiness." But leaning toward the second tightrope walker can lead to false humility or pride disguised as humility. By insisting they are just sinners with desperately sick hearts, these people can claim to be humble while maintaining an excuse to continue to sin. But this professed humility is false. Saying "look how humble I am" is still a subtle form of pride.

So what's true humility? It is when we place all our confidence in what Christ has done for us. It's when we "glory in Christ Jesus, and . . . put no confidence in the flesh" (Philippians 3:3). Paul says, "Let no one keep defrauding you of your prize by delighting in self-abasement" (Colossians 2:18, *NASB*). God is not trying to rub our noses in our sin. That doesn't give Him any pleasure. The only thing that gave Him pleasure was His Son's perfect sacrifice for our sins. Now through that sacrifice, He is at work restoring us as fallen human beings and building us up so that we become like Christ.

The whole point of the circus illustration is to remind us that we need to stay humble and balanced. If just one of the tightrope walkers is shouldering us, then our view of sanctification will lead toward some form of legalism. Legalism is when we care about rules and how things are done more than we care about showing love to God's people.

Paul said, "For I am confident of this very thing, that He who began a good work in you will perfect it until the day of Christ Jesus" (Philippians 1:6, *NASB*). If *truth* is the means by which we are set apart (sanctified), then *faith* is the means by which truth is gathered up through thought and action.

Where are you today in your walk? Are you riding on the shoulders of one of the extremes? Or are you in the center where there is balance and peace? Take some time today to think about your walk. Remember, you are sanctified; you are being sanctified; and one day, you will be glorified. It may seem hard to believe, but all of that is true of you.

Discussion

- The Bible clearly speaks of the believer's sanctification in what three ways?
- Our tendency to claim holiness and overlook sin, and the necessity to assume responsibility for our growth, leads to what?

- Humility in Christ is always found in the center of the tightrope. What happens if we tip toward the ends of the tightrope?
- Where are you on the tightrope?
- How can you adjust your position to gain balance and peace?

The Lie to Reject

I reject the lie that I am set apart (sanctified) by anything other than truth.

The Truth to Accept

Truth is the means by which I am set apart (sanctified).

Prayer

Dear heavenly Father, You said that I'm marked with a seal—the promised Holy Spirit—who guarantees my inheritance in Christ. Lord, help me look to the truth that will set me free so that I can follow You and do Your will. In Jesus' name I pray. Amen.

Reading

1 Corinthians 2:1-16

Without Faith!

Without faith it is impossible to please God.
Hebrews 11:6

If someone asked you, "What's faith?" how would you answer? Every part of your life is affected by how you answer that question. What do you believe in? What do you put your trust in? For the Christian there is only one answer—the person of Jesus Christ.

He is the One in whom we put our faith. And it is that faith that brings salvation to our lives. We are saved by faith: "It is by grace you have been saved, through faith" (Ephesians 2:8). And second, we walk or "live by faith, not by sight" (2 Corinthians 5:7). Faith is the only way that we can experience God and get to know Him better. Faith will play the greatest role in shaping our lives as we become more like Christ. So it is absolutely essential that we understand what true faith is. Read the following story about faith:

> The fields were parched and brown from lack of rain, and the crops lay wilting from thirst. People were anxious and irritable as they searched the sky for any sign of relief. Days turned into arid weeks. No rain came.
>
> The ministers of the local churches called for an hour of prayer in the town square the following Saturday. They requested that everyone bring an object of faith for inspiration. At high noon on the appointed Saturday the townspeople turned out en masse, filling the square with anxious faces and hopeful hearts. The ministers were touched to see the variety of objects clutched in prayerful hands—holy books, crosses, rosaries.
>
> When the hour ended, as if on magical command, a soft rain began to fall. Cheers swept the crowd as they held their treasured objects high in gratitude and praise. From the middle of the crowd one faith symbol seemed to overshadow all the others: A small nine-year-old child had brought an umbrella.[3]

Now that's real faith!

Do you want to become more like Jesus, do His will and follow the leading of His Spirit? If so, what you're seeking is an intimate walk of faith with Jesus. To see that that happens, you need to understand three important principles about faith.

1. Faith Is Dependent on Its Object

Everyone in the world has faith in something, whether it's Buddha, a fat bank account, oneself or Jesus. Every one of us has an object of faith. When we think of faith, the big issue isn't whether we believe, or even how much we believe, the real issue is, in whom are we putting our trust? The only difference between the Christian and the non-Christian isn't faith. The difference is the object of their faith. If you have the wrong object for your faith, then nothing in your spiritual life will go right.

The HMS *Titanic* was the most expensive, most luxurious cruise liner of its day. It boasted the most modern innovations that humans had ever devised. It was so advanced that its makers called it "The Unsinkable Ship." But sadly, as you know, on its maiden voyage the unsinkable soon became the unthinkable, as the *Titanic* sank and hundreds of passengers lost their lives in the icy waters of the Atlantic. The *Titanic* was the object of every passenger's faith. Every person who walked that gangplank was putting his or her trust in the safety and soundness of that vessel. Did you know that there were passengers who booked passage on the *Titanic* but canceled their travel plans when they heard that the shipping line had boasted that the *Titanic* was unsinkable? Believing that the shipping line was mocking God, some passengers refused to go on board. As it turns out, their lack of faith in the *Titanic* saved their lives.

It's amazing what people will put their faith in even when it involves their safety and life-and-death circumstances. Not many of us travel by ship anymore, but like those early travelers, we're putting our trust and our faith in planes, trains and automobiles—and in a hundred different objects every day. If we put that much trust in things made by mere men, how much more faith should we have in Jesus Christ, who said, "I am the way and the truth and the life" (John 14:6)?

What makes Jesus Christ the only legitimate object of our faith? We find the answer in Hebrews 13:7-8: "Remember your leaders, who spoke the word of God to you. Consider the outcome of their way of life and imitate their faith. Jesus Christ is the same yesterday and today and forever." These verses in Hebrews don't tell us to imitate our leaders' actions but rather to have the same kind of faith that our leaders have. Why is that? It's because their actions are the result of what they believe. Because they believe in God and they put their trust in Christ, their actions will be good.

What if the *Titanic* never sank? Would it then be a good object of your faith? How long would it be a good object of your faith? You might be asking, "Where are you going with this?" Well, even if the *Titanic* had successfully sailed for 100 years, eventually its steel hull would deteriorate. So the *Titanic* could never be a permanent object of our faith. But the Bible says in Hebrews that Jesus Christ is the same today, yesterday and forever. Because Jesus never changes, that makes Him the only sound and eternal object for our faith. Every other object of our faith is going to sink eventually. Only One sails on forever—Jesus Christ.

Since we've been talking about transportation, let's stick to the same theme to make this next point. Your faith grows in something as it shows itself to be dependable. Have you noticed how we don't travel by dirigibles, like the *Hindenburg*? At one time, people thought traveling overseas in a helium balloon, high amongst the clouds, would be the ultimate in traveling pleasure. But after about a half dozen dirigibles burst into flames and crashed to the ground, people weren't about to get on board, even if others paid their way. Why? They had lost their confidence, or faith, in that object.

But God has proven Himself over the course of time as an unwavering object worthy of our faith. The Bible tells us that the only trustworthy object of our faith is the person of Christ. You can't just have faith in faith. Faith has no power without Jesus Christ. So what is the object of your faith?

2. Our Faith Is Determined by How Well We Know the Object of Our Faith

Romans 10:17 says, "Faith comes from hearing the message, and the message is heard through the word of Christ." It's a simple equation: The better we know God and His Word, the greater faith we will have.

If we try to live a life of faith beyond what we know or understand to be true from the Word of God, it will only lead to failure and frustration. If we wing it, and just believe whatever we want to believe about God rather than looking in the Bible to see what it says about Him, we are setting ourselves up for deception and a real faith crisis. We'll be devastated when God doesn't do what we wanted Him to do or behave the way we thought He should behave. We'll lose our confidence in Him and our faith will grow weak. But the problem wouldn't be God's faithfulness but our false beliefs about Him that undermine our faith. So we can't assume anything is true. To discover the truth we have to find it in the Word of God. Some people, when they read the Bible, say, "Oh, I can't believe that!" But, of course, they can. If they couldn't believe it, God wouldn't ask them to. If one person can believe the truth, then everyone can.

What you believe is up to you. It's your choice, and no one can make that choice for you. Faith is something you decide in your mind. It is not a choice made by your emotions. It may not even be something you feel like doing. But, if you believe in something true, you can decide to believe it with your mind.

Joshua said, "If serving the Lord seems undesirable to you, then choose for yourselves this day whom you will serve. . . . But as for me and my household, we will serve the Lord" (Joshua 24:15). "Elijah went before the people and said, 'How long will you waver between two opinions? If the Lord is God, follow him; but if Baal is God, follow him'" (1 Kings 18:21).

We will never become more like Jesus without trusting God and His Word. Our sanctification depends on whom or what we choose to believe. Do we want to be great men and women of God? Every great follower of Jesus trusted God and His Word. They let the Word of God speak into their lives and determine what they believed and how they behaved. What was truth and what was a lie? What was right and what was wrong? To them, the Word of God was the source of life.

Are you trusting in God's Word, or are you determining in your own mind what you think is true? First Corinthians 1:25 says, "the foolishness of God is wiser than man's wisdom, and the weakness of God is stronger than man's strength."

3. The Bible Presents Faith as an Action Word

Real faith leads to action. Let's go back to the *Titanic* for a second. Who were the people who put their trust in the *Titanic*? The answer is simple—those that got on board. Their faith was not well founded. They put their faith in an unsound object, and it led to a negative result. But if you put your faith in something sound, you'll get a positive action. This is what James is trying to get across when he says, "What good is it, my brothers, if a man claims to have faith but has no deeds? Can such faith save him? But someone will say, 'You have faith; I have deeds.' Show me your faith without deeds, and I will show you my faith by what I do" (James 2:14,18).

He makes an even stronger statement later: "A person is justified by what he does and not by faith alone" (James 2:24). Does that mean that we aren't saved by faith and faith alone? No! In the Bible, the English words "faith," "trust" and "belief" all come from the same Greek noun. In common English usage, however, to believe in something has less personal commitment than to trust in something. It is easy to give mental assent by saying "I believe that" and totally miss the biblical meaning of belief. Biblical faith is not just giving mental assent to something; biblical faith requires full reliance upon it.

We can believe in our minds that the *Titanic* will float, but we do not trust it until we get on board. It's amazing how easily people were convinced about the safety of the *Titanic* and were willing to put their trust in a man-made object. Yet we seem to struggle with trusting God who has always shown Himself to be reliable. It's easy to say, "I'm trusting God." However, are we really depending on Him? James said, "You believe that there is one God. Good! Even the demons believe that—and shudder" (James 2:19). What is James's point? He's saying that even the demons believe and know that there is a God, but we won't see them in heaven because they do not trust in Him. Only when our faith manifests as action does it truly affect how we live and show itself in our sanctification.

For example, Jesus said, "Blessed are those who hunger and thirst for righteousness, for they shall be satisfied" (Matthew 5:6, *NASB*). Do you believe that? If you do, then you must be hungering after righteousness.

If you aren't doing that, then your belief is only wishful thinking, which will neither save you nor sanctify you.

Life would be terribly confusing if we had to search and search to find a sound vessel that would help us sail through life. As the *Titanic* has taught us, one bad voyage is all it takes. God's Word makes clear what is truth and what is a lie. Incidentally, we don't have the privilege or the right to determine for ourselves what it is that we are to believe. We as believers choose to believe the truth; we don't choose what truth is.

Jesus said He is "the way and the truth and the life" (John 14:6). Through our prayers and reading of God's Word, God reveals His truth to us. He can reveal the truth, show us the way and give us the life that we need in order to follow Him. Truth originates in heaven, and our responsibility is to believe it.

What do you believe about God? How do you know if it is true? Write down some of your beliefs; then see if they line up with Scripture. If they do, keep on believing. If they don't, don't beat yourself up: Simply choose to believe what the Bible says and walk in that new truth.

Discussion

- What's the only difference between the Christian and non-Christian when it comes to faith?
- What makes Jesus Christ the only legitimate object of our faith?
- Is faith something you *decide* to do or something you *feel* like doing?
- What do faith, trust and belief have in common?
- Where does truth originate? What is our responsibility regarding truth?

The Lie to Reject

I reject the lie that having faith is something I *feel* like doing.

The Truth to Accept

I accept the truth that having faith is something I *decide* to do.

Prayer

Dear heavenly Father, You said that Your Son, Jesus, is the same yesterday, today and forever [see Hebrews 13:8]. *I know I can trust Him and that He is the only reliable object of my faith. Lord, I believe You know what's best for me. Help me to walk by faith and not by sight. In Jesus' name I pray. Amen.*

Reading

1 Corinthians 3:1-9

Hearts Filled with Truth

*And the peace of God, which transcends
all understanding, will guard your hearts and
minds in Christ Jesus.*
Philippians 4:7

Yesterday we talked a lot about faith—the kind of faith that will actually change our character. We discovered that faith means putting our trust in the truth, allowing it to change us. Let's take a look at how choosing to believe the truth about how we belong to God changed a person's life in a profound way:

> My mother wasn't married when I was born so I had a hard time. When I started to go to school, my classmates had a name for me and it wasn't a very nice name. I would go off by myself at recess and during lunchtime because the taunts of my playmates cut so deeply.
>
> What was worse was going downtown on Saturday afternoon and feeling every eye burning a hole through me. They were all wondering just who my earthly father was. When I was about twelve years old, a new preacher came to our church. I would always go in late and slip out early. But one day the preacher said the benediction so I got caught and had to walk out with the crowd. I could feel every eye in church on me. Just about the time I got to the door, I felt a big hand on my shoulder. I looked up and the preacher was looking right at me.
>
> "Who are you, son? Whose boy are you?"
>
> I felt the old weight come on me. It was like a big, black cloud. Even the preacher was putting me down.
>
> But as he looked down at me, studying my face he began to smile a big smile of recognition. "Wait a minute," he said, "I know who you are. I see the family resemblance. You are a son of God."
>
> With that he slapped me across the rump and said, "Boy, you've got a great inheritance. Go and claim it!" That was the most important single sentence ever said to me.[4]

Like the person in the story, we all need to let the truth of how we belong to God's family sink deep into our hearts. Whatever God is calling us to believe, whether it's a truth about Christ or our identity in Him, we need to have a level of trust that is beyond our understanding.

God wants us to have a faith that everyone can see. Paul put it this way: "Let the peace of Christ rule in your hearts" (Colossians 3:15). Do you know what "rule" means? Have you ever watched a baseball game? When the umpire makes a call at the plate, he's making a ruling. Is the pitch a ball or a strike? He makes the call. Just like an umpire, we are to let the peace of Christ make the call in our lives. If the peace of God is to be the umpire of our lives, then it is obvious that God's truth needs to be firmly planted in our minds. Like the umpire's rulebook, it needs to be in place so that we can experience God's peace. The passage in Colossians goes on: "Let the word of Christ dwell in you richly as you teach and admonish one another with all wisdom" (Colossians 3:16). The words "let" and "dwell" mean "to inhabit."[5] *What* or *who* is Paul saying should take up residence in our hearts? The Word of Christ—the truth that centers on Christ is to be at the very core of our beings. We are to let His peace make the call like the umpire at a baseball game. Apart from Christ we don't naturally know right from wrong. When it comes to matters of the heart, we need an umpire (the Word) to guide us. Everyone has an opinion on every issue in life. The world has an opinion, the flesh has an opinion, and the devil has an opinion. If we listen to these opinions, we're headed for bondage. What we want is God's opinion, because He never lies to or misleads us.

I (Dave) was the first person in my family to accept Christ as Savior. As I began to get into God's Word and renew my mind, a battle began. The enemy wasn't about to give up the ground he had gained in my life before I knew Christ. Before I knew Christ, I didn't care what I let into my mind; and after I accepted Christ, the enemy wanted to use those things to control me.

If we have no peace, we sense a constant battle for our minds, and sometimes it's tempting to give up because we get battle weary. The Bible tells us exactly what to do in those tough times. We are told to submit to God and resist the devil (see James 4:7). If we are battle weary, it's probably because we've been fighting with our own fleshly strength. We need to remember that "the weapons we fight with are not the weapons of the world. On the contrary, they have divine power to demolish strongholds" (2 Corinthians 10:4). We need the peace of God to guard our hearts and minds (see Philippians 4:7).

Imagine your mind is like your car. Lately you've been driving wherever you want, going down some pretty dirty and sinful roads. One day you decide that you want to get back on the right path with Jesus. You realize that your car is in pretty tough shape, so you take it to the car wash. You have your car detailed inside and out. All the stains, the mud and grime, smashed bugs and road rash are washed away. That car wash is just like the Word of God.

We need to go to the Word to have our minds washed, renewed and cleansed every day. But we need to do more. If we continue to travel down those old roads, it won't take 10 minutes for the car to get as dirty as it was before. We need to choose new pathways. It's hard. The old pathways seem shorter; we know them well and they have been convenient. But given time, we'll get to know the new clean pathways and they will seem more familiar. We'll still need to go to the Word of God Car Wash, but it will seem more like hot wax and polish than a mud bath. Our cars (our minds) will stay clean provided we go down the right path and wash them regularly.

That illustration reinforces what we learned earlier about the part we play in our own sanctification. The apostle Paul says, "Do your best to present yourself to God as one approved, a workman who does not need to be ashamed and who correctly handles the word of truth" (2 Timothy 2:15). There is no substitute for studying and meditating on God's Word. God will not study for us. He has revealed Himself and His ways in His Word, and it is our responsibility to know the truth. According to Scripture, meditation is a sure way to let the Word of God richly dwell within us. Let's see what we can learn about the discipline of meditation in biblical history.

Studying God's truth is one of the most important tools we have when it comes to living like Jesus. Joshua 1:8 says that meditating on God's Word is the key to successful living: "Do not let this Book of the Law depart from your mouth; meditate on it day and night, so that you may be careful to do everything written in it. Then you will be prosperous and successful." This verse is asking us to do two things: do what God's Word says and meditate on His truth. If we do these two things, the Bible says we will be wise and successful.

To make sure our hearts stay filled with truth, there are certain things that we must do and certain things we must avoid. First, we must be careful whom we listen to and what kind of advice we take. If I hide God's Word in my heart but then let my evil friends talk me into sin, I'm not truly letting God's Word take control of my mind. "What partnership have righteousness and lawlessness, or what fellowship has light with darkness?" (2 Corinthians 6:14, *NASB*).

So are you partying with saints or sinners? If you party with saints, you will be built up. If you party with sinners, you will probably do what they are doing. "Do not be misled: 'Bad company corrupts good character'" (1 Corinthians 15:33).

We also aren't to make fun of or mock the Word of God and righteousness. Some people find those who are living for Jesus to be easy targets for their cute jokes. But we need to realize that those who are meditating on God's Word are really blessed. The Bible says, "He is like a tree planted by streams of water, which yields its fruit in season and whose leaf does not wither. Whatever he does prospers" (Psalm 1:3).

Hiding God's Word in your heart is a big deal to God. In Deuteronomy 6:6-9 (*NASB*) we read:

> These words, which I am commanding you today, shall be on your heart. You shall teach them diligently to your sons and shall talk of them when you sit in your house and when you walk by the way and when you lie down and when you rise up. You shall bind them as a sign on your hand and they shall be as frontals on your forehead. You shall write them on the doorposts of your house and on your gates.

In other words, no matter what you are doing or where you are doing it, you are to meditate on God's Word. It is to be a part of your life every minute of every day.

If we meditate on God's Word every day, it will affect all those around us—friends at school, sisters and brothers, moms and dads, coaches and teachers. God is concerned about our cities, our homes and what our hands are doing. All three of those things are talked about in Deuteronomy.

Psalm 63 reveals King David in a very depressing situation. He is on the western shore of the Dead Sea, which is described as "a dry and weary land where there is no water" (v. 1). This wilderness area is the same place where Satan confronted our Savior. Throughout Scripture we find that the wilderness is a place of trial and temptation. In this psalm, bleak surroundings alone are depressing, but far worse is the reason for David's presence there. He is fleeing for his life. He is either fleeing from Saul or one of Absalom's sons who is attempting to wrest the kingship of Israel from him (scholars disagree on the exact time). But David's heart is strong toward God even in the midst of his circumstances. How is that possible? Because David meditates on God's truth:

> O God, you are my God, earnestly I seek you; my soul thirsts for you, my body longs for you, in a dry and weary land where there is no water. Because your love is better than life, my lips will glorify you. I will praise you as long as I live, and in your name I will lift up my hands. My soul will be satisfied as with the richest of foods; with singing lips my mouth will praise you. On my bed I remember you; I think of you [or meditate on you] through the watches of the night (Psalm 63:1,3-6).

Life is pretty tough, and sadly you won't have to wait very long to use the technique that David used to bring peace to his heart. David recalled all of his great times with God. He recounted all the times God had blessed him, protected him or cared for him. Then David used those moments to direct himself toward worship. There were times David raised his hands and even laid on the ground before God.

When you feel the pressures of life, think on Jesus. If you need to, try raising your hands or even singing. Remember, God doesn't care if you can carry a tune. He just wants you to worship Him and meditate on His truth. Don't be surprised if your troubled mind experiences a noticeable feeling of comfort and peace. God may not change your circumstances, but you will find that He will give you the comfort you need to make it through. "Why are you in despair, O my soul? And why are you disturbed within me? Hope in God, for I shall again praise Him, the help of my countenance and my God" (Psalm 43:5, *NASB*).

If you are struggling today with a particular issue in your life, don't be afraid to ask others to help you find a specific portion of God's Word that will be help you renew your mind in that area. Don't tough it out alone. The Body of Christ is supposed to be a family. Let others pray for you and help you discover God's powerful truth, which will set you free.

Discussion

- The faith that will actually change our character and our behavior involves believing and putting our trust in what?
- Paul said, "Let the peace of Christ rule in your hearts" (Colossians 3:15). What does the word "rule" mean in this verse?
- The words "let" and "dwell" are one word in the original Greek text. What do they mean?
- What is a sure way to let the Word of God richly dwell within you?

The Lie to Reject

I reject the lie that bad situations can take over my life.

The Truth to Accept

I accept the truth that no matter how I feel, I can always meditate on my God's incredible ways and His Word.

Prayer

Dear heavenly Father, You are my God. My soul thirsts for You, my body longs for You, even in a dry and weary land. Because Your love is better than life, I will glorify You. I will praise You as long as I live, and in Your name I will lift up my hands. I will think of You and meditate on Your glory and provision every day. In Jesus' name I pray. Amen.

Reading

1 Corinthians 3:10-23

Meditation

Be transformed by the renewing of your mind. . . .
Think so as to have sound judgment.
Romans 12:2-3, *NASB*

Meditation may not seem like a very important component in your Christian life, but without it, there is no successful way to navigate through life. When the Bible talks about meditation, it usually has two meanings. First, it means to speak. Although we can meditate in our minds, the idea here is to say out loud God's truth or His Word so that it fills our minds.

We see the power of words when we realize that we can sing along with a song on the radio after hearing it only two or three times. In the same way, we are to meditate on God's truth. The second meaning of "meditation" refers to repeating something in one's mind several times. Some might think, *That sounds too hard, or it will take up too much time.* But the Bible tells us plainly that we won't be transformed or changed or even become like Christ unless we renew our minds. It is like the story of the missing hyphen. It is a true story that shows the importance of the small things in our lives.

Sometime ago a newspaper headline read, "Missing Hyphen Blamed in Rocket Failure."

It was hard to believe that a small hyphen in a computer readout caused the destruction of a huge, powerful missile.

Perhaps you've heard the old proverb: "For want of a nail a horseshoe was lost; for want of a horseshoe, a rider was lost; for want of a rider, a battle was lost; for want of a battle, a war was lost." The loss of the war, in other words, was connected to the loss of a nail.

Apparently, that was the case here. On the day in question, a Venus space probe launch vehicle, boosted by an eighteen-million-dollar U.S. Atlas rocket, was lost because a hyphen was missing from a computer equation.

Richard Morrison, a NASA official, told the House Space Committee investigating the incident that the missing hyphen caused a mathematical miscue.

Said Morrison, "The hyphen gives a cue for the spacecraft to ignore the data the computer feeds it until radar contact is once again restored. When that hyphen is left out, false information is fed into the spacecraft control systems. In this case, the comput-er fed in hard left, nose down, and the vehicle obeyed." Who left out the hyphen? Morrison either didn't know or wasn't saying, but he speculated that it was the mistake of some senior official with advanced degrees and a Ph.D. in celestial navigation.

There is an important hyphen that belongs in your life, too. It doesn't seem like much, but without it, you can crash. That hyphen *is time alone with God.* A time to pray, a time to read God's Word, a time to listen to God's voice. Just a few minutes a day is all it takes to keep our lives on course.[6]

Meditation, like that hyphen, needs to have the proper place in our lives.

Since this is a daily devotional, let's put some truth into action. Let's take Romans 8:1 (*NASB*): "There is therefore now no condemnation for those who are in Christ Jesus." Notice that this verse doesn't say, "There is little or even less condemnation for those who are in Christ Jesus." The verse says, "There isn't any," meaning that at no time, if we are in Christ, can anyone or anything successfully bring a condemning charge against us that can separate us from who we are in Christ. Think about the word "condemnation." Condemnation is a kind of punishment, or condemn-ing charge. Oftentimes we as believers experience false guilt and mental attacks from the enemy, or we subject ourselves to self-talk and put our-selves down. But according to this verse, that is not from Christ. There is no condemnation or punishment for those who are in Christ Jesus. What is amazing is there are no restrictions put on us other than that we be "in Christ" to be free from condemnation.

That is just a single verse, 13 small words, but you can still see the prac-tical value of meditating on those truths. If you hide that truth in your heart, you will not receive the enemy's next attack. Romans 8:1 is one example of how powerful and practical God's Word is. God's Word can bring comfort and direction to your life when it penetrates your heart.

A few days back we talked about faith. We said faith had to have an object. In the same way, the object of our meditation is just as impor-tant. It wouldn't do us any good if we meditated on a lie. That would only tear us down and weaken our Christian walk. God's Word reminds us in 1 Timothy 4:1: "The Spirit clearly says that in later times some will abandon the faith and follow deceiving spirits and things taught by demons."

The enemies of the Lord Jesus Christ are never happier than when a follower of Jesus chooses to believe a lie and meditates on something that is just not true. So many young people aren't rehearsing what is true, but sadly they rehearse the lies again and again in their mind. Things like "I'm no good," or "I can't do anything right" are repeated again and again in their minds. This doesn't help them improve; rather, it is the enemy's way of wearing believers down and deceiving them so that they eventually live like people who seem to do everything wrong.

God wants us to be very careful with our minds. What we see and hear and dwell on will soon become a common subject in our minds. If it is truth, we'll walk in the light of that truth. If it's a lie, we'll struggle in the darkness of deception. God never bypasses our minds. He works through our minds. We aren't to let our minds go blank or meditate on nothingness as some would suggest. Rather, we are to focus on real truth that affects our lives in a practical way. "Brothers, stop thinking like children. In regard to evil be infants, but in your thinking be adults" (1 Corinthians 14:20). "Be transformed by the renewing of your mind. . . . Think so as to have sound judgment" (Romans 12:2-3, *NASB*).

In the false religions of the world, the big idea behind many acts of meditation is to put a person's mind in neutral. In transcendental meditation, for example, people are to sit in a quiet room, shut their eyes tightly and repeat special words or phrases over and over again. Repeating this mantra for 20 minutes or more is supposed to put one in a trance in which his or her mind is shut off and out of contact with the rest of his or her being. This type of meditation wants us to get our minds out of the way so that we can experience "truth" directly. But nowhere in the Bible are we told to meditate in this way. Jesus warned us about praying in vain repetitions (see Matthew 6:7). In fact, 2 Corinthians 10:5 (*NASB*) asks us to do exactly the opposite. It tells us to take "every thought captive to the obedience of Christ."

Thinking wrong thoughts can lead to despair, with which even some great Christians have even struggled. Jeremiah became depressed when he reflected on all his hardships: "I remember my affliction and my wandering, the bitterness and the gall. I well remember them, and my soul is downcast within me" (Lamentations 3:19-20). He had lost hope in God. It would be depressing to "well remember" all the negative things that have happened to us while thinking about all the evil in this world. But Jeremiah turns everything around: "Yet this I call to mind and therefore I have hope: Because of the Lord's great love we are not consumed, for his compassions never fail. They are new every morning; great is your faithfulness" (Lamentations 3:21-23). Notice that nothing changed in Jeremiah's circumstances, and God never changed. All that changed was what Jeremiah *chose to believe* in God. **Note:** God's truth was already *in his mind.* He only had to recall what he already knew of God.

The apostle Paul experienced his tough times as well—everything from shipwreck to imprisonment. Yet, this is what he told the believers in Philippi to meditate on: "Finally, brothers, whatever is true, whatever is noble, whatever is right, whatever is pure, whatever is lovely, whatever is admirable—if anything is excellent or praiseworthy—think about such things. Whatever you have learned or received or heard from me, or seen in me—put it into practice. And the God of peace will be with you" (Philippians 4:8-9). The *New American Standard Bible* translates this phrase as "dwell on these things."

When I (Dave) used to wrestle, I was trained to respond to the moves of my opponent. I had to respond quickly and at a moment's notice or I would end up on my back, defeated. In the same way, Paul isn't talking about things in life that don't matter. He's referring to the process of disciplining our minds to think truthfully, carefully and comprehensively so that when Satan tries to move in on us, we can counter his move with truth. This is not merely trying to remember a Bible verse when we're tempted or in trouble as if it were some magic formula. This is learning to think biblically about everything in life so that we can avoid being pinned and defeated. Are you winning your wrestling matches today? If you're not, start meditating on God's truth. It is a surefire way to turn defeat into victory.

Discussion

- What does it mean to meditate on the Word of God?
- What are the two forms of meditation?
- What is the value of meditating upon God's Word?
- Why can encouraging people to meditate without telling them what to meditate on be spiritually destructive?
- Meditation is learning to think biblically about what?

The Lie to Reject

I reject the lie that life is hopeless and meaningless.

The Truth to Accept

I accept the truth that no matter how bad my circumstances may appear, God is in control of my life!

Prayer

Dear heavenly Father, Your Word says to think about noble, right, pure, lovely, excellent and praiseworthy things. Lord, help me to focus on You and Your Word. You said that whatever I have learned, received or heard from You, I should put into practice and I would have Your peace! I want Your peace, so I choose to put into practice all that You have taught me. In Jesus' name I pray. Amen.

Reading

1 Corinthians 4:1-5

Meditation and Actions

*Finally, brothers, whatever is true, whatever is noble,
whatever is right, whatever is pure, whatever is lovely,
whatever is admirable—if anything is excellent or
praiseworthy—think about such things.*
Philippians 4:8

Life is hard. It's not always easy to have a positive attitude and to find the perspective that is right, lovely and pure. When we get hurt or bad things happen to us, it's easy to think about problems and bad circumstances. But God's Word tells us to choose a different path—to think on what's true and excellent. This true story illustrates this point:

> Not a lot of press coverage was given to the tough Argentine golfer Robert De Vincenzo, but one story from his life shows his greatness as a person.
>
> After winning a tournament, De Vincenzo received his check on the eighteenth green, flashed a smile for the camera, and then walked alone to the clubhouse. As he went to his car, he was approached by a sad-eyed young woman who said to him, "It's a good day for you, but I have a baby with an incurable disease. It's of the blood and the doctors say she will die." De Vincenzo paused and then asked, "May I help your little girl?" He then took out a pen, endorsed his winning check, and then pressed it into her hand. "Make some good days for the baby," he said.
>
> A week later as he was having lunch at the country club, a Professional Golfer's Association official approached him, saying, "Some of the boys in the parking lot told me you met a young woman after you won the tournament." De Vincenzo nodded. The official said, "Well, she's a phony. She has no sick baby. She fleeced you, my friend."
>
> The golfer looked up and asked, "You mean that there is no baby who is dying without hope?" This time the PGA official nodded. De Vincenzo grinned and said, "That's the best news I've heard all day."[7]

Do you see how De Vincenzo chose to focus on what was good? He chose that lovely and excellent path that Philippians 4:8 talked about.

Colossians 3:1-2 says, "Since . . . you have been raised with Christ, set your hearts on things above, where Christ is seated at the right hand of

God. Set your minds on things above, not on earthly things." The golfer in the story truly had a heavenly perspective. He didn't care about the money he lost, as so many in the world might. Instead, he found joy in the fact that there was no suffering child.

Whatever we think about and let our minds dwell on eventually filters into the depths of our heart. Soon our thoughts become part of our actions. What would happen if we decided to think like Jesus and embrace His truth in every area of life? It is obvious that we would soon be living and acting like Jesus. "The good man brings good things out of the good stored up in his heart, and the evil man brings evil things out of the evil stored up in his heart. For out of the overflow of his heart his mouth speaks" (Luke 6:45).

The third king to rule over Israel was said to be the wisest man ever to live. He was so wise because he had asked God for wisdom. His name was Solomon, and even though he was wise, he made many mistakes. But when he asked the Lord for a discerning heart, he was literally asking for "a hearing heart," or a heart that hears God's Word so that he could judge the people rightly (see 1 Kings 3:9). How much time each day do we spend watching TV or listening to music? Is what we watch and listen to something Jesus would take in? We can't expect to have the mind of Christ after spending 20 minutes in God's Word and 4 or 5 hours filling our minds with negative images.

Have you taken an English class in which you studied Shakespeare? In addition to a lot of thees and thous, you might have also run across something called a soliloquy. Whether you're reading *Macbeth* or something else, a soliloquy is always the same. It simply means talking to oneself.

The Bible often instructs us and gives us examples of people who talk to themselves to bring their focus back on God and His truths. It's like telling ourselves to "get a grip" or "relax." Notice the psalmist does that exact thing: "Find rest, O my soul, in God alone; my hope comes from him" (Psalm 62:5) and "Praise the Lord, O my soul; all my inmost being, praise his holy name" (Psalm 103:1). When we talk to ourselves, it may look and sound goofy, but it's a great teacher if the truth is from God's Word or consistent with it.

What should we think on first? Obviously it needs to be the person of Christ. God is to be the center and focus of our lives. He is our King and creator, and our hearts should focus on Him. Nothing else should captivate our mind and attention like God. When you think about God, do His greatness, mercy and love inspire a sense of awe in your life? It should. We are called not just to think about God but also to worship Him. To worship Him is to reflect on all of His awesome attributes. Meditation is meant to lead us not just to study cold facts about a distant God but rather to lead us to a closeness and fellowship with an intimate God of love. Meditation awakens our relationship with God so that we can truly experience what it means to be children of God. This truly allows God's Word to come alive in our hearts.

Look at what the psalmist meditated upon:

On his law he meditates day and night (Psalm 1:2).

We meditate on your unfailing love (Psalm 48:9).

I will meditate on all your works (Psalm 77:12).

I meditate on your precepts (Psalm 119:15).

I will meditate on your wonders (Psalm 119:27).

I meditate on your decrees (Psalm 119:48).

I meditate on [your law] all day long (Psalm 119:97).

I meditate on your statutes (Psalm 119:99).

I may meditate on your promises (Psalm 119:148).

I meditate on all your works (Psalm 143:5).

Remember the golfer in the story? He wasn't directly meditating on God, but he was thinking about something that was good. In addition to God and His attributes, we're to think about whatever is good. We're not saying that we should pretend that nothing bad ever happens to us. We need to keep in touch with reality. But like the golfer, we need to choose a positive perspective that allows us to walk in joy rather than bitterness and defeat. Sometimes that is hard. When we're weak, we are spiritually tired. If that is where we are, we need to listen to these words from Matthew 11:28: "Come to me, all you who are weary and burdened, and I will give you rest."

If you know a trial or tough time is just around the corner, don't wait until you are in the middle of it to prepare your mind. Meditate before the event occurs, so you will be more likely to respond the way Jesus would respond in that situation. That's what 1 Peter 1:13 reminds us to do: "Prepare your minds for action; be self-controlled; set your hope fully on the grace to be given you when Jesus Christ is revealed."

Say you've been reading God's Word and you discover that Christians aren't supposed to marry unbelievers. You realize that your boyfriend or girlfriend isn't a believer. You feel as if the Holy Spirit is directing you to break off that relationship. Meditating on God's truth can help you get through this emotionally charged time. You are called to prepare your mind for action no matter what the issue in life is.

Will you make God the center of your thoughts today? If you do, you won't regret it.

Discussion

- Whatever we meditate on goes into our hearts and affects what?
- Whatever reaches into the depth of our being will come out in which two ways?
- Solomon asked God for a "discerning heart." What was he literally asking for?
- Beyond God and His ways, we should meditate on what?
- There is nothing wrong with visualizing yourself doing something in the power of the Holy Spirit, provided that your thoughts are consistent with what?

The Lie to Reject

I reject the lie that it is too difficult to concentrate or meditate on God regularly.

The Truth to Accept

I accept the truth that I can prepare my mind for action and have greater self-control through meditation.

Prayer

Dear heavenly Father, You said that to prepare my mind for action I should be self-controlled and set my hope fully on Jesus Christ. Lord, I know that when I do this I will have greater self-control and victory in my life. Lord, I praise Your name and Your ways. In Jesus' name I pray. Amen.

Reading

1 Corinthians 4:6-21

Truth, Jesus and You!

The Word became flesh and made his dwelling among us.

John 1:14

Today's verse can sound a little mysterious. The "Word became flesh" refers to the Word of God, or Jesus, becoming man. Jesus is exactly what truth looks like when it takes human form. God wants us to understand truth so that it can fill our minds and display itself in our lives the same way it did in the life of Christ. When we believe the truth, we will fall in love with God and humankind. We will desire the things God desires.

I (Dave) had the opportunity to visit Auschwitz. The cold barbed wire and evil gas chambers are embedded in my mind to this day. The crimes against humanity that occurred there boggle the mind and demonstrate the horrible power of evil in this world. Yet, in the midst of all the evil and darkness, it is amazing how even the smallest light can breach the dark. For all the ugly memories of Auschwitz, there is one of beauty. It's the memory that a man named Francis Gajowniczek has of Maximilian Kolbe.

In February, 1941, Kolbe was incarcerated at Auschwitz. He was a Franciscan priest. In the harshness of the slaughterhouse he maintained the gentleness of Christ. He shared his food. He gave up his bunk. He prayed for his captors. One could call him the "Saint of Auschwitz."

In July of that same year there was an escape from the prison. It was the custom at Auschwitz to kill ten prisoners for every one who escaped. All the prisoners would be gathered in the courtyard and the commandant would randomly select ten men from the ranks. These victims would be immediately taken to a cell where they would receive no food or water until they died.

The commandant begins his selection. At each selection another prisoner steps forward to fill the sinister quota. The tenth name he calls is Gajowniczek.

As the SS officers check the numbers of the condemned, one of the condemned begins to sob. "My wife and my children," he weeps.

The officers turn as they hear movement among the prisoners. The guards raise their rifles. The dogs tense, anticipating a command to attack. A prisoner has left his row and is pushing his way to the front.

It is Kolbe. No fear on his face. No hesitancy in his step. The capo shouts at him to stop or be shot. "I want to talk to the commander," he says calmly. For some reason the officer doesn't club or kill him. Kolbe stops a few paces from the commandant, removes his hat and looks the German officer in the eye.

"Herr Kommandant, I wish to make a request, please."

That no one shot him is a miracle.

"I want to die in the place of this prisoner." He pointed at the sobbing Gajowniczek. The audacious request is presented without stammer.

"I have no wife and children. Besides, I am old and not good for anything. He's in better condition." Kolbe knew well the Nazi mentality.

"Who are you?" the officer asks.

"A Catholic priest."

The block is stunned. The commandant, uncharacteristically speechless. After a moment, he barks, "Request granted."

Prisoners were never allowed to speak. Gajowniczek says, "I could only thank him with my eyes. I was stunned and could hardly grasp what was going on. The immensity of it: I, the condemned, am to live and someone else willingly and voluntarily offers his life for me—a stranger. Is this some dream?"

The Saint of Auschwitz outlived the other nine. In fact, he didn't die of thirst or starvation. He died only after poison was injected into his veins. It was August 14, 1941.

Gajowniczek survived the Holocaust. He made his way back to his hometown. Every year, however, he goes back to Auschwitz. Every August 14 he goes back to say thank you to the man who died in his place.

In his backyard there is a plaque. A plaque he carved with his own hands. A tribute to Maximilian Kolbe—the man who died so he could live.[8]

How could Kolbe make such a sacrifice? How could he have no regard for his own life and freely surrender it for another? Kolbe held a

Christlike truth in his heart that transformed every fiber of his being. This is what all of God's truth is to do in our lives. It is less than Christian of us to say that we know the Word of God when it has not touched our hearts nor transformed our character. When truth is appropriated, it touches every aspect of the heart.

The truth in Kolbe's life touched even the deepest parts of his heart. Nothing else can explain his unselfish love for a complete stranger. Psalm 104:34 says, "May my meditation be pleasing to him, as I rejoice in the Lord."

Meditation not only affects our actions as it did Kolbe's, but it also affects every part of our lives, including our emotions. Both our thoughts and feelings are joined to our hearts. So, if truth reaches our hearts, it should also reach our emotions. Then the truth of God's Word will truly change our lives and our actions.

Our emotions are triggered by our thought life. We aren't really shaped by the external events in our lives as much as we are by how we perceive them. Kolbe was willing to die in the man's place because he could relate to the man's need to be with his family. His heart and emotions were moved with compassion. His emotions weren't the product of his circumstances but rather a product of the truth in his life. In other words, Kolbe didn't think, *Oh no, I'm going to die!* Truth told him that he would be with Christ. So he was willing to surrender this life so that the man could live and be reunited with his family.

The truth directed Kolbe's life, and it must direct ours as believers in Christ. Let's hope you'll never be faced with the terrible dilemma that Kolbe had to face, but every decision you make in life has eternal consequences. Sadly, there are thousands of Christians who would never even consider making Kolbe's sacrifice if they were in his exact circumstance. Christians who have let Satan's lies affect their minds and their emotions find it difficult to view life from God's heavenly perspective. They have inappropriate feelings about themselves and God. Sadly, just telling some people the truth will not necessarily resolve their problems. The primary obstacle to accepting biblical truth is a lack of genuine repentance along with unresolved personal and spiritual conflicts.

Bitterness due to lack of forgiveness is the biggest hurdle for most people to overcome. Many teens have discovered that repenting from sin, pride, rebellion, bitterness and deception results in a freedom that they had never experienced. When they resolved their conflicts, they were able to joyfully connect with their heavenly Father. Those who are free in Christ have a peace guarding their hearts and their minds. They know who they are as children of God because the Holy Spirit is bearing witness with their spirits. The emotional impact of all this can be seen on their faces. Before they resolved their conflicts, the Holy Spirit was being quenched, but now the Spirit of truth is bearing witness in repentant hearts.

One of the most common results of finding freedom in Christ is that our emotions and true feelings come alive. Paul said, "I now rejoice, not that you were made sorrowful, but that you were made sorrowful to the point of repentance; for you were made sorrowful according to the will of God, in order that you might not suffer loss in anything through us. For the sorrow that is according to the will of God produces a repentance without regret" (2 Corinthians 7:9-10, *NASB*).

I have seen young people feel sorry about their past or feel sorry that they shared about their pasts with others. But I have never seen anyone feel sorry after he or she repented. The conviction of sin produces the sorrow that leads to repentance without regret. True inner peace is the result of complete repentance.

Discussion

- If we know the Word of God, then it has touched what two areas of our lives?
- God's Word will not change our lives unless it changes what?
- Our emotions are the product of our thought lives. We are not shaped so much by external events as we are by what?
- What is true inner peace the result of?

The Lie to Reject

I reject the lie that God's Word cannot change my life and emotions.

The Truth to Accept

I accept the truth that God's Word will change my life and my emotions.

Prayer

Dear heavenly Father, the apostle Paul said he rejoiced because the people he led to You were made sorrowful to the point of repentance. The sorrow that is according to the will of God produces repentance without regret. Lord, I don't want sorrow in my life; but if it removes sin from my life, I know it's for the best. Help me to be so quick to turn from sin that sorrow will have no place in my life. In Jesus' name I pray. Amen.

Reading

1 Corinthians 5

Meditation
Methods

*My son, keep your father's commands and do not
forsake your mother's teaching. Bind them upon your heart
forever; fasten them around your neck. When you walk, they
will guide you; when you sleep, they will watch over you;
when you awake, they will speak to you.*

Proverbs 6:20-22

When we think about how God feels about us, and His incredible power, we see all that He put in place so that He could have a relationship with us. This should cause us to want to put all of our confidence in Him. As a songwriter and student of God's Word King David meditated often. Most of the time, he simply wrote down his feelings: "My soul clings to you; your right hand upholds me" (Psalm 63:8). King David had his fair share of troubles. No matter what the circumstances, he didn't turn his back on God, even though God tested him. There were times when David was driven into the wilderness by evil armies. Still, David's soul held on to God in the midst of the darkest of times. David never forgot that God loved him. He had seen God's love in the past and that love had left an indelible message in his heart and his mind. David refused to be discouraged by the dark times. Rather, he focused on God's past faithfulness and loving kindness, and the truth of His Word, to determine how he would act and feel. Through meditation, David recalled again and again how God was taking care of him. We are no different from David, and we need to let God's Word have the same powerful effect in our lives.

God is always at work in our lives. He's always with us. Because of His presence, we always have the power we need to live above our circumstances and experience peace in the midst of stormy times. We're not talking about painting on a smile like some clown in a circus. We're talking about power that gives us inner joy and real strength. Studying God's Word and meditating on His truth ready us to face whatever the world, our flesh or the devil can throw at us. Proverbs 6:20-22, today's opening Scripture passage, tells us that meditating on the truth will prepare us for all of life's circumstances.

God's Word is meant not only to guide us but also to correct us when we believe a lie or behave badly. In the Psalms it says, "How can a young man keep his way pure? By living according to your word. I seek you with all my heart; do not let me stray from your commands. I have hidden your word in my heart that I might not sin against you" (Psalm 119:9-11).

The meditation that the world teaches is focused on emptying our minds and thinking about nothing. But Christian meditation has a real purpose and focus. We are to think about the person of Christ and His truth. We are to practice that truth and go over it in our minds until it finally reaches our hearts and completely controls our minds, emotions and wills. Let's get practical. How can we practice Christian meditation? Here are a few ideas.

1. Personalize the Truth

You may feel funny at first, like you are rewriting the Bible or something, but here's a way to make God's Word very personal in your own life. Place your name in the verse you are studying. For example, Hebrews 13:5 (*NASB*) says, "I will never desert you, nor will I ever forsake you." Say to yourself, "God will never desert me nor will He ever forsake me."

You could also try this with Jesus' words from John 14:1-3 (*NASB*): "Do not let your heart be troubled [your name]; believe in God, believe also in Me [your name]. In My Father's house are many dwelling places; if it were not so, I would not have told you [your name]; for I go to prepare a place for you [your name]. If I go and prepare a place for you, I will come again and receive you to Myself [your name], that where I am, there you [your name] may be also."

It's kind of cool, as if Jesus were personally talking to us. Sometimes it is easy for us to read God's Word and not get involved with it or apply it to our lives. We can go to church and youth group, and it's like we aren't really there. But it is our responsibility to sing the choruses and to think about what they mean—to sing them from our hearts. When we hear a message, God expects us to personally apply it. God isn't concerned with how much factual information we gather up in our minds about Him; rather, He wants our knowledge of him to affect how we think and speak and love. Anything less is just sick and dead religion.

2. Visualize the Truth

The Bible gives us many word pictures. What kind of mental picture comes to your mind after reading Romans 14:1-3?

Now, try to picture heaven and what it might be like. What's the most significant thing about going to heaven? How do you feel knowing that

God loves you so much that He's prepared a special place for you and you will be with Him for all eternity?

3. Respond to the Truth

Have you ever watched people as they sang a chorus about lifting their hands to the Lord and no one was lifting their hands? Doesn't that make you feel funny? We're supposed to respond to God's Word. If God's Word calls for praise, then stop and praise Him. If you really want to hide God's Word in your heart, then you have to respond to whatever it calls you to do. If God's Word talks about wisdom, ask for wisdom. If God's Word talks about prayer, take time to pray. If God's Word reveals a sin, be quick to confess it. Proverbs 28:13 says: "He who conceals his sins does not prosper, but whoever confesses and renounces them finds mercy."

God's truth expects obedience. Jesus said, "If you love Me, you will keep My commandments" (John 14:15, *NASB*). James says, "Do not merely listen to the word, and so deceive yourselves. Do what it says. Anyone who listens to the word but does not do what it says is like a man who looks at his face in a mirror and, after looking at himself, goes away and immediately forgets what he looks like. But the man who looks intently into the perfect law that gives freedom, and continues to do this, not forgetting what he has heard, but doing it—he will be blessed in what he does" (1:22-25).

4. Let God's Word Transform You

There is a big difference between information and transformation. When we get to heaven, we won't be rewarded if we answer all the questions right on some heavenly Bible quiz. Our reward will come from the areas of our life that have been transformed by the power of God's Word. Are we more loving than when we first came to Christ? Are we kinder? Can people see Christ in us? We can know a lot of Bible facts, but we will never be powerful witnesses for Christ if His gospel doesn't change our hearts and our love for the lost. God's Word must reach our emotions as well as our behavior.

5. Meditate on the Word to Strengthen Your Relationship with the Author

Meditating on God's Word also helps us hear His voice and discern His leading. John 10:3 says that His sheep will hear His voice. If what we think we are hearing from God doesn't match His Word, we know that that voice is not from God. God's guidance is always consistent with His Word. If our relationship with God has been strengthened through meditation, we will be quick to discern a lie of the enemy from the comforting voice of our Savior and Lord. The Word is food for our souls. In fact, it is like water. We can go quite a long time without food, but we won't last very long without water. Meditating on God's Word satisfies the thirst of our souls and allows God to take His truth into our hearts—the very wellspring of our lives. It's from that wellspring that we can draw the strength we need to live out the life of Christ. Drink up!

Discussion

- What is Christian meditation?
- Through meditation, God's truth finally reaches what? What two things does meditation affect?
- What do we receive from the words we meditate on?
- What are the five practical methods of meditation?
- Using a passage from the last eight days, go through the five steps of meditation. Be sure to personalize what you visualize.

The Lie to Reject

I reject the lie that I can merely please God by listening to the Word.

The Truth to Accept

I accept the truth that I should do what the Word says!

Prayer

Dear heavenly Father, I know that meditating on Your Word will give me a sharper awareness and a better appreciation of Your greatness. Keep me faithful and help me come to Your truth for wisdom and understanding every day. Help me store what I learn deep in my heart so that I can stand strong in You whatever the circumstances of my life. I need You to conform me to the image of Christ. I pray in His precious and powerful name. Amen.

Reading

1 Corinthians 6:1-8

The Power of Our Actions

For this reason, since the day we heard about you, we have not stopped praying for you and asking God to fill you with the knowledge of his will through all spiritual wisdom and understanding. And we pray this in order that you may live a life worthy of the Lord and may please him in every way: bearing fruit in every good work, growing in the knowledge of God, being strengthened with all power according to his glorious might so that you may have great endurance and patience, and joyfully giving thanks to the Father, who has qualified you to share in the inheritance of the saints in the kingdom of light.

Colossians 1:9-12

Don't you wish that you could just stay a kid and not have any responsibilities? It wouldn't be very practical. After all, you wouldn't want your parents to have to drive you to a movie when you are 35. Well, God doesn't want us to stay immature either. God's Word teaches us how to grow up. Paul revealed this cycle of growth in Colossians 1:9-12.

I (Dave) remember wanting to grow up so bad, and I looked forward to the day when I would have whiskers on my face. I don't know, I guess I thought whiskers were the ultimate sign of being a man. I even remember praying and asking God for whiskers. Well, God answered my prayer and now I have so many whiskers, if I don't shave every day, I turn into a wolf man. When we are young, we don't always pray for the things we should and our focus is not always the same as God's focus. Paul shares how we can grow up and he gives us several foundational elements, which we have listed in the following diagram.

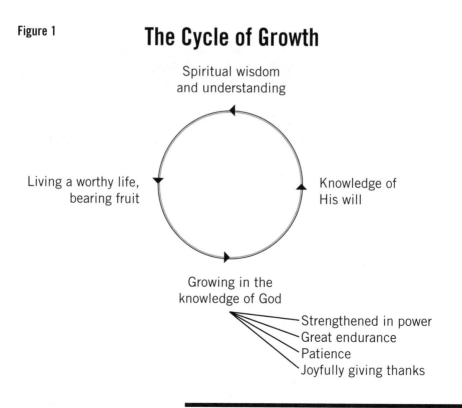

Figure 1

The Cycle of Growth

Spiritual wisdom
and understanding

Living a worthy life,
bearing fruit

Knowledge of
His will

Growing in the
knowledge of God

Strengthened in power
Great endurance
Patience
Joyfully giving thanks

The process of growth begins with the knowledge of God's will, which we will find—guess where? I hope you said, "The Bible." If you didn't, read the last three days over again! God's truth must go deep in our hearts for us to have a Christlike understanding of how truth applies in our lives. The cycle isn't complete, however, until we make the choice to live out what we know to be true from His Word. A real walk of faith comes when we display a humble and submissive life of obedience to God and His Word. When we live in this way, we start to grow up. The things we have learned about God bring us back to where we started. In other words, we will receive greater knowledge as we act on the knowledge we already have. As a result of this growth, our friends and family will see more spiritual strength, endurance, patience, joy and thankfulness, which become increasingly evident in our character.

We can mess up our growth cycle at any of the four points in figure 1. We could mess up stage 1 by reading the Bible as if it were some boring textbook, never allowing its truth to touch our hearts. We'd have facts but no real wisdom or understanding of God or what was at the heart of the life of Christ.

At the stage 2, God's truth tackles our heart. As a result, it shines a light on any darkness it may find there, convicting us of even the smallest sin. This gives us very personal wisdom and direction for life. But we could construct a roadblock and stop the whole process of growth if we never confessed our sin and showed the fruits of repentance. At stage 2, God may ask us to do things we've never done before, such as witness to a lost friend. Some natural roadblocks may come up—and if we don't know God's Word, we won't know how to get around them. The most common roadblock here is fear, sometimes a fear of failure or rejection. Fear of anything other than God can tear down our faith. That is why we are to encourage one another, "For God did not give us a spirit of timidity, but a spirit of power, of love and of self-discipline" (2 Timothy 1:7).

In stage 3, our experiences come into play. We begin to gain understanding as we walk by faith and experience the joy of bearing fruit in our Christian walk. This positive growth encourages us to grow even more. Here is where we can see a real acceleration in our Christian walks.

Because of this walk of faith, we gain maturity and understand God's Word as we never have before.

A word of warning though: If you fail to live by faith, not only will you fail to bear fruit, but your negative experiences can cause you to lose ground. In the Christian life, you don't just stop growing. You are either moving forward or you are falling backward. That is why you have to decide to live by faith.

Finally, we can stop the process of growth at stage 4 by failing to come back to the Word of God. One of the great dangers of successfully bearing fruit or experiencing victory is that we might decide to rest in our past experiences. We are tempted to think that we have arrived. That's why Paul's encouragement in Philippians 3:12-14 is so helpful:

> Not that I have already obtained all this, or have already been made perfect, but I press on to take hold of that for which Christ Jesus took hold of me. Brothers, I do not consider myself yet to have taken hold of it. But one thing I do: Forgetting what is behind and straining toward what is ahead, I press on toward the goal to win the prize for which God has called me heavenward in Christ Jesus.

The life of an athlete illustrates the process of growth we're talking about—especially if it's the life of a Christian athlete like Eric Liddell. Read his story and see if you can spot the four cycles of growth:

> Saturday, July 5, 1924, was the day for the eighth Olympiad of modern time to begin. Amid the waving and cheering there came the skirl of the pipes, and the Queen's Cameron Highlanders emerged from the gateway. They were an impressive sight in their swinging kilts and bearskin headdresses. For a moment the crowd seemed mesmerized at the sight and sound, but when the team from Great Britain came marching in behind the band, the cheers rang out even louder. . . .
>
> All this while Eric Liddell was coming under a lot of pressure to run in the 100 meters. Really it hadn't stopped when months

earlier he said he wouldn't run on a Sunday. But once in Paris the criticism began to hurt more.

Eric went to see Harold Abrahams, Britain's remaining hope for a medal in the 100 meters, and he wished him well. As a Jew, Harold's Sabbath was Saturday and Eric respected this. He understood that it was as right for Harold to run on a Sunday as it would have been wrong for himself.

Sunday, July 6, saw the young Cambridge University student Abrahams lined up for the 100-meter preliminary heat. At the same time, Eric Liddell was addressing a congregation in the Scots Kirk (church) on the other side of Paris.

Harold came through both heats. The following day he was all set for the semifinal, and among the spectators was Eric to cheer him on to victory.

Deep inside, Eric must have felt a time of regret—but there wasn't an element of envy in him. He was elated for Harold's success.

Now he felt free of the criticism too and was able to concentrate on his own two events. The 200-meter heats were held on Tuesday. Both Eric and Harold qualified in each for a place in the final the next day.

But when Thursday came and the 400-meter heats, Eric didn't do too badly. He didn't shine, either, even though his time improved in each heat. It was better still the next in the semifinal. Still, he only managed to qualify. On the previous day, in one heat, Imbach of Switzerland actually broke the world record when he ran the distance in 48 seconds.

There were six finalists: two Americans, one Canadian, and the two Britishers, Guy Butler and Eric Liddell. . . .

As usual, Eric went along the line shaking the competitors' hands and giving them his best wishes. This was a ritual the international crowd had begun to look for although they still thought it strange to see one sportsman wishing his rival well—but they didn't know Eric the man.

In the last few moments before the gun, as the athletes were warming up, without any warning a mighty sound filled the enormous arena. The pipes and drums of the Queen's Cameron Highlanders had struck up with "The Campbells Are Coming."

The British team organizer, Sir Philip Christison, had sensed some despondency among the British supporters and thought some rousing music would cheer them up. Maybe it would spur Eric Liddell too. After all, he was a Scot and the skirl of the pipes would surely send the blood racing through his veins just at time when it was most needed.

Eventually the music faded. A tense silence returned only to be shattered by the sharp crack of the starting pistol, and Eric was off.

No one could believe what they were seeing. Right from the start he leapt into a three-meter lead. Everyone knew that he couldn't keep up that pace. A 100-meter man couldn't do what he was doing. Still, he pounded on. Guy Butler was running his heart out, too. For a while the crowd seemed hypnotized. Then the unexpected occurred. Fitch, one of the Americans, overtook Butler to sprint closer and closer to Eric who was still in the lead. But again the unexpected happened. Eric began to run faster.

Closer and closer he drew to the tape—without seeing it. His head was back on his shoulders and his eyes were looking up to heaven. From out of nowhere, it seemed, hosts of British Union Jacks appeared among the onlookers to wave him on to victory.

Suddenly, after what seemed like miles, the 400-meter race was over. Eric Liddell reached the tape a full five meters ahead of Fitch, with the injured Guy Butler sprinting into third place to take a bronze.

The crowd's roar could be heard all over Paris. Then, in a brief spell of quiet, a voice boomed out over the speaker to announce that Eric had run the race in a new world record time of 47.6 seconds. This time it seemed the cheers would be heard across the channel in Britain.

Sir Philip Christison was confident the stirring effect of the pipes and drums had spurred the 22-year-old Scot to victory that day. But Eric knew it was something quite different. It was all due to a few simple words written on a scrap of paper.

In the days leading up to his races, the masseur officially assigned to care for the British team had come to know Eric very well and he liked him immensely.

To try in some way to show the athlete how much he admired him, as Eric was leaving his hotel for the Colombes Stadium, the masseur came up to him and pressed a piece of folded paper into his hand.

Later, in one of the few quiet times of that day, he unfolded the paper and read: "In the old book it says, 'He that honors me I will honor.' Wishing you the best of success always."

For the 1924 Olympic Games a motto had been especially created. It was "Citius, Althius, Fortius," meaning "Faster, Higher, Stronger," and it could apply to no competitor more than to Eric Liddell.[9]

But Eric Liddell's story didn't stop there. After his great Olympic victory, he chose a course seldom traveled, one where there where no banners waving or crowds cheering his name. Eric knew he had been born to run, but he also knew he had been born to serve. Eric's knowledge of God and His plans controlled everything he did, and it controlled when he would run and why. God was preparing Eric for an even greater race, the race of life. Eric looked to God alone to see what the future held for him. He heard the world call to him—after all, he was an Olympic champion—but Eric didn't listen to that call. Instead, he responded to a still, small voice, the voice of God. God's will and God's Word had shaped Eric, and his calling or choice for the future was clear.

So Eric Liddell entered the ministry and served as a missionary far away from cameras and news headlines.

Discussion

- What does the process of growth begin with?
- Living by faith requires us to exercise our will. Name two ways we can do this.

- What are some of the stages and results of the growth cycle?
- The growth cycle can be blocked at what four points in the diagram?
- One of the great dangers of successfully bearing fruit or experiencing victory is that we might decide to what? Why?

The Lie to Reject

I reject the lie that I have arrived spiritually and don't need to grow.

The Truth to Accept

I accept the truth that I can grow each day in strength, patience and joy!

Prayer

Dear heavenly Father, I want to live a life worthy of You. I want to please You in every way and bear fruit. Help me grow in the knowledge of Your ways. I pray that You will strengthen me with all power according to Jesus' glorious might so that I may have great endurance and patience. In Jesus' name I pray. Amen.

Reading

1 Corinthians 6:9-20

Changing the Heart

*Now that you know these things, you will be
blessed if you do them.*
John 13:17

Sometimes when people change their minds, they'll say that they've had a change of heart. When we say that someone has had a change of heart, we are saying that that person has changed his or her thoughts or beliefs about something. As followers of Jesus, we are to let the truth of God's Word sink into our hearts so deeply that it grabs hold of our emotional core. We are to let the truth affect not only our emotions but our actions as well. Take a look at how truth affects our emotions and then flows to our actions in figure 2.

Figure 2

The Primary Flow

Thoughts ⟶   Emotions ⟶   Actions ⟶

You are at a point in your life when you are making a lot of important choices. These choices will affect the course of your entire life. If your actions are based on improper thoughts and emotions, then it is obvious that your actions or choices won't be good ones. Listen to the importance of having the right beliefs from one of your peers. Sara Ann Zinn of Crook County Christian School understood the importance of believing the truth and how it would affect her choices. Check out what she said at her graduation.

> As graduating seniors we are faced with choices. Now is the time that we who once were children begin making decisions as adults.
>
> The solid foundation of our Christian education and the forming of our beliefs and our character by this school and our families, have prepared us for the journey ahead.

Some of us have already chosen the avenue that will lead to our goals and dreams—others are still at the crossroads. Some will go to college, some will get married and start families, some will go off to defend our nation, while others will immediately enter the workforce. Whatever choices we make, we must always remember who we are and what we represent.

The road is long, and the journey is rough,
At times it seems hard to find strength enough.
But through it all, the ups and downs,
We learn to smile despite the frowns.
We learn to share our joy and pain,
To share without expecting gain.
We learn to give a helping hand
And how to lean when we can't stand.
We learn the difference between right and wrong
To stand for right, and always stand strong.
Though this road is hard and seems so long
It's how we find where we belong;
Because it's only through life's bends and turns
That we can truly grow and truly learn.[10]

It's important that we, like Sara, discover how our behavior influences both our thoughts and emotions. How can our behavior affect our thoughts and emotions? That can happen because all three—our thoughts, emotions and actions—are tied together in our heart. Most of us respond from our feelings. But the Bible is telling us, we don't feel our way into good behavior; rather, we behave our way into good feelings. One of the biggest issues among students is bitterness and lack of forgiveness. When we have been deeply hurt by someone, we often don't feel like forgiving him or her. Yet God's Word clearly commands us to forgive. In other words, we are to make the choice with our mind and go through the act of forgiveness and then in time, our feelings may change. If we wait until we feel like forgiving, we may never forgive. We will continue to live in disobedience to God's Word and in bondage to bitterness in our lives. We'll be prisoners to our own emotions. God's Word is telling us that the act of forgiveness will eventually lead to emotional freedom.

We can actually will ourselves out of certain moods, just as David did when he was depressed: "I have trusted in Your lovingkindness; my heart shall rejoice in Your salvation. I will sing to the Lord, because He has dealt bountifully with me" (Psalm 13:5-6, *NASB*). Let's look at what David did to overcome his depression. First, he focused on God and how awesome He was. Then David expressed confidence that his heart would rejoice. David probably wasn't jumping up and down right away, but he knew in his mind that good times would come. So he made the choice to sing as he recalled all the times that God had been good to him.

When has God been good to you? Do you remember when He saved you? Can you recall a specific prayer that He answered? When you feel like your emotions have been run over by a Mack truck, do what David did—recall to your mind the goodness of God. Are you worried that we're going to ask you to start singing? Well, you're right. And even if you are not a singer, you could play a Christian CD that will build you up. If you have been listening to dark music and getting verbally trashed by your friends, don't be surprised if you're feeling down. We're called to listen to truth. Start focusing on what God says about you. Listen to positive music. Start smiling.

The Bible, when it talks about our emotions and how we are to feel, commands us to be happy—to rejoice and be filled with joy. Oftentimes the commands of God are viewed in a negative light. But there is nothing that you should dislike about this command. The command to be happy sounds pretty good to us. There are other commandments about showing love, having peace and not giving in to fear. All this raises a question: How are we to obey those biblical commands? If we cannot change our emotions directly, what can we do to change them?

Remember that we said that our emotions are linked to our thoughts. The Word of God tells us that we can transform our emotions by placing in our minds positive truths. The Bible also tells us that we can change our emotions by changing our actions. By acting or behaving in a certain way, we can change our emotions.

Figure 3

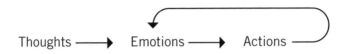

Actions Affect Emotions

Thoughts ⟶ Emotions ⟶ Actions

When the Bible commands us to love one another, it isn't talking about the emotional feelings of love. It's addressing the action of genuine love. If our emotions and wills are truly connected in the depths of our hearts, then a sincere act must effect a change in our emotions. To put it simply, the doing of an act of kindness or love also creates the emotion of love. Doing the loving thing based on God's Word will eventually connect emotionally in our hearts. That will be true only if there are no unresolved conflicts caused by not speaking the truth in love and no failures to forgive from the heart. Is there anyone in your life that you're having a hard time loving? If so, remember not to focus on your emotions but to center on God's command to love. Give it a try. Rejoice, and most of all, love. Jesus told His first followers that people would know that they were His followers because of their great love for each other! Be a loving follower of Jesus today.

Discussion

- Changing the heart begins with a change of what?
- When truth penetrates the heart, it touches our emotional core, which motivates us to do what?
- Read Genesis 4:6-7. How does the biblical account of Cain and Abel show that an action can change how we feel?

- True or false:
  We don't always feel our way into good behavior. ____
  We behave our way into good feelings. ____
  The Bible teaches that we change our emotions by changing our
     actions. ____

The Lie to Reject

I reject the lie that love and compassion are based on feelings.

The Truth to Accept

I accept the truth that the Bible teaches that we change our emotions by changing our actions.

Prayer

Dear heavenly Father, when King David wasn't happy he trusted in Your loving kindness, rejoiced in Your love and praised You for Your bountiful provision. Lord, I confess that often when I feel down I don't want to thank or praise You. Help me look past the present by saying "I love You, I trust You, and You have been kind to me." Then, like David, I know happier feelings will follow. In Jesus' name I pray. Amen.

Reading

1 Corinthians 7:1-9

Our Actions Affect
Our Thoughts

*Now for this very reason also, applying all diligence,
in your faith supply moral excellence, and in your moral
excellence, knowledge; and in your knowledge, self-control,
and in your self-control, perseverance, and in your perseverance,
godliness; and in your godliness, brotherly kindness,
and in your brotherly kindness, love.*
2 Peter 1:5-7, *NASB*

If our thoughts, emotions and actions are all interconnected in our hearts, then our actions must also affect our thoughts and beliefs.

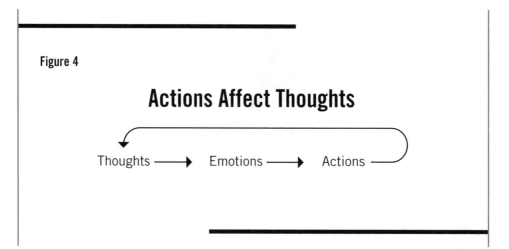

Figure 4

Actions Affect Thoughts

Thoughts ⟶ Emotions ⟶ Actions

This truth is displayed in our everyday lives as well as presented in the Bible. Let me (Neil) illustrate. In a spiritual conversation with a young lady, I found out that she wanted to believe in the existence of God. But she said, "I just can't get myself to do it." I went through my usual biblical points proving the existence of God, but nothing I said seemed to convince her. No amount of proof seemed to leave an impression in her mind. So I simply told her that since she wanted to believe in God, she should live as though God was real. She took my advice. I saw her again about 12 months later, and I could hardly believe the change. Her choice to live like a follower of Jesus had worked its way into her beliefs. Now she was a true believer, and her decision to live as a Christian was just what she needed to become one.

I suppose if a person thought of him- or herself as a gangster, a rough and rugged criminal, he or she would soon find him- or herself a member of a gang of like-minded people living out a life of crime. If a person lives out a certain role, that lifestyle will become imprinted on his or her thinking and that mind-set will truly affect that person's actions.

If you begin to act more mature and grown-up, that mind-set will work its way into your self-perception and guess what? You will actually become more mature. For example, in one study, young girl smokers who role-played the emotional life of a lung cancer victim cut back their smoking more than those who were simply given information about the hazards of smoking.

Thoughts and actions are not only tied together in certain biblical terms, they are also linked in the teachings of the Bible. After assuring us that God's divine power has granted us everything pertaining to life and godliness (see 2 Peter 1:3), and that we have been made partakers of the divine nature (see 2 Peter 1:4), Peter then shares our role:

> Now for this very reason also, applying all diligence, in your faith supply moral excellence, and in your moral excellence, knowledge, and in your knowledge, self-control, and in your self-control, perseverance, and in your perseverance, godliness, and in your godliness, brotherly kindness, and in your brotherly kindness, love (2 Peter 1:5-7, *NASB*).

The most important foundational building block to our character is faith. We will never demonstrate love or have solid character if our faith isn't in the right place. The building block of faith affects the deepest part of who we are and what we do. If we believe a lie, then everything that shows up in our life will be out of sorts because it is linked to something false. We can't do anything without first thinking or believing it, which means that all of our actions come from our thoughts. This is how our body works. Our central nervous system was meant to operate in this way. We won't pour a cold drink without first thinking about it. It is our responsibility to choose to believe all the truths of God's Word and let those truths form our character. In other words, what we say and do is determined by what we believe.

God calls us to obey Him 100 percent of the time. Oftentimes we want to know what God is up to before we'll commit to obey Him, but that is rebellion. The *only* appropriate response to faith in God is to act on it—and then you will know why. You don't have to know why in order to trust and obey, but there is a good chance that you will know why if you have been faithful. The knowledge gained from the experience of trusting and obeying leads to greater self-control, which eventually is perfected in love. The understanding of love is borne out in our actions:

> This is how we know what love is: Jesus Christ laid down his life for us. And we ought to lay down our lives for our brothers. If anyone has material possessions and sees his brother in need but has no pity on him, how can the love of God be in him? Dear children, let us not love with words or tongue but with actions and in truth (1 John 3:16-18).

The Bible also makes it clear that to know love, we must actually experience love. We must be loving people. The apostle John says:

> We have come to know and have believed the love which God has for us. God is love, and the one who abides in love abides in God, and God abides in him. If someone says, "I love God," and hates his brother, he is a liar; for the one who does not love his brother whom he has seen, cannot love God whom he has not seen (1 John 4:16,20, *NASB*).

Our experiential actions of love lead us to the real knowledge of love. No one would say that Mother Teresa of Calcutta didn't understand love. Her actions were too great. In fact, she inspired thousands of others to follow her example of love. A young boy wrote a letter to Mother Teresa asking how he could make a difference with his life, as she had with hers. For months he didn't hear anything from her. Then one day he received a letter from Calcutta, India. He expectantly opened it up and read four words that changed his life:

> Find your own Calcutta.
> —*Mother Teresa*[11]

We all have to find our own Calcutta. We can't just think about it—we have to grab the opportunity to reach out and love someone. Where is your Calcutta? Your friends? Your school? You only have a brief window of opportunity to reach many of them. Are you ready? Love leads to action, which leads to a deeper knowledge of love and God's provision.

At our Stomping Out the Darkness student conferences, we talked with hundreds of young people who expressed the desire to follow Jesus. Yet their personal lives were riddled with bondage, and they were struggling with habitual sin in a number of areas. It was obvious that something was wrong with their belief systems. Somewhere tucked away in their perception of God or their view of themselves were lies that were undoubtedly being used by the world, the flesh and the devil to captivate and control their lives. But remember, Jesus said, "Whoever has my commands and obeys them, he is the one who loves me" (John 14:21).

On the other hand, we counsel hundreds of young people who aren't very lovely. In some instances we don't feel very close to them and we have to work at loving them. Yet it is always exciting when God works a miracle of love in our own hearts after we have done everything we can to help them. An emotional bond usually develops—a bond that comes by actively loving them by the grace of God.

John said, "Whoever lives by the truth comes into the light, so that it may be seen plainly that what he has done has been done through God" (John 3:21). In other words, truth is what a person does as well as what he knows and understands. The more we choose to live the truth, the more we come to know the truth. "If we claim to have fellowship with him yet walk in the darkness, we lie and do not live by the truth" (1 John 1:6). John also said he receives great joy from knowing that his friends are "walking in the truth" (2 John 4).

Jesus said, "If any man is willing to do His will, he shall know" (John 7:17, *NASB*). You'll have difficulty discerning God's will for your life if you first don't have a willing heart to do what He says. If you are willing to obey Him, no questions asked, then you almost always will know what His will is.

This is really true when it comes to God's guidance in our lives, because He guides us out of our obedience. For example, try steering a parked car. It's hard to turn the wheel isn't it? But when the car is rolling down the road, it can be easily maneuvered. It is the same way in our lives when we are on the move, walking in obedience to God's commands. He can easily steer us and make any corrections in the directions of our lives.

Until we decide to turn our whole lives and control over to God, then He really isn't our master and Lord. We need to understand that as God, He has the capacity to understand what is best for us and therefore knows what course our lives should take that would best conform us to the life of Christ. We must believe in our hearts that God's will is "good, pleasing and perfect," as Romans 12:2 tells us. According to that verse, the renewing of our minds will result in testing and proving that the will of God is best.

Discussion

- Faith is the foundation that leads us toward the ultimate character of what?
- What is the basis for all that we are and do?
- Name two things that happen when we choose to believe the truth and act accordingly.
- Why does knowledge follow moral excellence in Peter's progression toward love (see 2 Peter 1:5-7, *NASB*)?
- What does it mean to "find your own Calcutta"? Where is yours?

The Lie to Reject

I reject the lie that I can become mature by just intellectually studying the Bible.

The Truth to Accept

I accept the truth that maturity comes when I believe the truth and live it out in everyday life.

Prayer

Dear heavenly Father, I want to diligently apply myself to growing spiritually. I want to supply my faith with moral excellence, and I want to supply my moral excellence with more knowledge about who You are and who I am in Christ. Lord,

I want to have self-control and perseverance so that people around me know that I love You. I know that You have made me holy so that I can live in godliness, kindness and love. I choose to live out Your love today. In Jesus' name I pray. Amen.

Reading

1 Corinthians 7:10-24

Actions and Knowledge

*Fear God and keep his commandments, for this is
the whole duty of man.*
Ecclesiastes 12:13

Today we want to look at how our personal actions affect our thoughts. Proverbs 1:7 says, "The fear of the Lord is the beginning of knowledge." Fearing the Lord carries with it the idea that our awe of God displays itself in practical ways in our lives. In other words, there are certain things that we as Christians would never do because such things would offend our God. Our fear of the Lord dictates our actions. When this kind of awe for the Lord is in place in our belief system, the Bible says we have wisdom. Job said it this way, "The fear of the Lord—that is wisdom" (Job 28:28). When we live out in our daily lives what we believe in our hearts, our understanding, or wisdom, increases.

In the New Testament, the book of James talks a lot about works and how it affects our faith. James makes it clear in his writing that the Old Testament character Abraham acted in great faith when he showed his willingness to sacrifice his own son Isaac in obedience to God's command. James says this about Abraham's actions, "As a result of the works, faith was perfected" (James 2:22, *NASB*). The Bible makes a clear link between faith and works. When our faith is real, it should always produce a good work in our lives. We've talked about that flow in previous days. But James is saying that it can flow the other way as well. Our good deeds, or works of righteousness, can also greatly affect our faith.

Have you ever bungee jumped? If you have, your first time was probably the hardest. It was the greatest leap of faith. But when you did it a second time, most likely it wasn't quite the heart-pounding experience it was the first time. Why? Because the work of the first jump strengthened your faith—perfected it, if you will.

In the same way, we're called to perfect our Christian faith. Because our faith involves believing or trusting, we can say that we are exercising our faith whenever we're performing a good work. Just like bungee jumping, that good work brings about a change or an increase in our personal faith. Our actions perfect our faith. With each act of obedience to God, we add a new layer of understanding of God and His ways, or we strengthen what we already know to be true of Him.

Unless we let the truth of God sink deep into our hearts, we will never grow in our Christian character. One of the best ways to internalize truth is to act it out in our daily life, not just giving it our mental assent, but letting it affect our actions. Understanding the Bible doesn't necessarily transform our lives. But when we know God intimately and practice His truths, we actually increase in wisdom and knowledge of our personal God. If we truly want to have a change of heart in our lives and live as Jesus lived, we will let God change both our minds and our actions. It would be nice if we had direct command over our emotions, but we don't. We can, however, believe God's truth and walk in His ways, which helps us grow in our knowledge of Him and transforms the way we feel.

When I (Neil) was a young pastor, a dear old saint handed me a note on the way out of church that said, "It is one of life's great compensations that you cannot sincerely help another without helping yourself in the process." The Christian life is more than a set of beliefs; it is a skill. It is the skill of a wise person who knows how to live practically in the ways of God. Learning a skill involves both theoretical knowledge and the practice of that knowledge. In the same way, growing in the Christian life involves both right belief, or theoretical knowledge, about life *and* the knowledge that comes only through the practice of living that life.

So much of the Christian life is accepting and doing our duty. We don't need any special guidance to love our neighbor as ourselves or to be witnesses to the resurrected life within us. We dignify our calling and honor God when we show ourselves faithful in what He has entrusted to us. Our duty is not to see what lies dimly in the future but to do what clearly lies at hand. Solomon said, "Here is the conclusion of the matter: Fear God and keep his commandments, for this is the whole duty of man" (Ecclesiastes 12:13). Bob Benson wrote about "Duty's Dignity":

> Her name was Cissy. She was solid black, and even though there was some question as to her family tree, she was a fine dog. As a pup she had destroyed the required number of newspapers, shoes, and flowerbeds to reach her maturity.
>
> She had a fine litter of pups, seven to be exact, and it was something to watch her care for them. Who taught that little dog, so recently a pup herself, to care and feed, clean and protect those seven wiggling, squirming, yapping appetites rolled in fur? Who placed that look of intense pride, beaming happiness? Who

gave that air of dignity? God did. God made that little dog. And in His world He gave her a share, a place to fill, a task to perform—a duty that dignified.

All of God's creatures have dignity, but it is only reached through the doorway of duty. He made you to stand tall, walk straight, play fairly, love wholeheartedly—and every time you think the mean thought, do the "small" thing, you stoop beneath your dignity.

Oh God, make us to be too tall to be stooped, too straight to be crooked, too big to be small. Help us to do the tasks that ennoble, the duties that dignify.[12]

Discussion

- What is the first principle of wisdom?
- Why doesn't biblical knowledge alone change our lives?
- A change of heart includes both a change of mind and a change of what?
- The fear of the Lord is the beginning of what?
- If we want to grow in our spiritual life, what must we internalize?

The Lie to Reject

I reject the lie that I can be a mature Christian and not change my ungodly behaviors.

The Truth to Accept

I accept the truth that a change of heart includes both a change of mind and change of action.

Prayer

Dear heavenly Father, thank You for Your plan of sanctification, Your plan to make me more like Your Son. Please show me where I am blocking growth in that direction and what I need to do to grow. I realize that my actions are keys to spiritual growth, so I'm asking for Your help. Help me when I'm feeling unloved or depressed. Give me strength to choose to act lovingly toward my friends and family. I know that positive feelings will follow in time. My actions affect my feelings, my thoughts, my knowledge and my faith in You. Direct my paths so that I will do what is right. Show me the ways of Your love—I am willing to follow. I pray this in Jesus' name. Amen.

Reading

1 Corinthians 7:25-40

True Freedom Requires Balance

Such confidence as this is ours through Christ before God. Not that we are competent in ourselves to claim anything for ourselves, but our competence comes from God. He has made us competent as ministers of a new covenant—not of the letter but of the Spirit; for the letter kills, but the spirit gives life. . . . Now the Lord is the Spirit, and where the spirit of the Lord is, there is freedom. And we, who with unveiled faces all reflect the Lord's glory, are being transformed into his likeness with ever-increasing glory, which comes from the Lord, who is the Spirit.

2 Corinthians 3:4-6,17-18

Remember the tightrope illustration we talked about in Day 2? We need to have the same kind of balance in our lives when it comes to two important areas that relate to our freedom in Christ. A true sign of Christian maturity is when we are able to live out balanced lives. The two extremes that we need to avoid when it comes to our freedom are legalism and license. Paul discusses, in Romans 6:1-11, how we are identified with Christ in His death, burial and resurrection. He says in verse 7, "Anyone who has died has been freed from sin." Every Christian has died with Christ and is, therefore, free from sin. However, Paul adds in Galatians 5:1-2, "It is for freedom that Christ has set us free. Stand firm, then, and do not let yourselves be burdened again by a yoke of slavery. Mark my words! I, Paul, tell you that if you let yourselves be circumcised, Christ will be of no value to you at all."

Now that we are free in Christ, the Bible tells us not to turn back to the old ways of the Law. Otherwise we would get trapped in a lifestyle that cares more about how things are done rather than the condition of our hearts. It also says that we shouldn't go to the other extreme and just commit any sin we like, believing that it doesn't affect our fellowship with God. We are called to be responsible and to avoid the two extremes of legalism and license.

When we embrace either extreme we develop patterns in our lives that can easily become habits or strongholds. Here is a riddle for you. Don't worry, it is not too hard.

> I am your constant companion.
> I am your greatest helper or heaviest burden.
> I will push you onward or drag you down to failure.
> I am completely at your command.
> Half the things you do might just as well be turned
>   over to me and I will be able to do them quickly and correctly.
> I am easily managed—you must merely be firm with me.
> Show me exactly how you want something done
>   and after a few lessons I will do it automatically.
> I am the servant of all great people and, alas, of all failures, as well.
> Those who are great, I have made great.

Those who are failures, I have made failures.
I am not a machine, though I work with all the precision
   of a machine plus the intelligence of a person.
You may run me for profit or run me for ruin—it makes no dif-
   ference to me.
Take me, train me, be firm with me,
   and I will place the world at your feet.
Be easy with me and I will destroy you.
Who am I?
I am Habit![13]

Every believer who has put his or her trust in Christ has become a child of God and is therefore positionally proclaimed through the blood of Christ to be free. But how many young Christians are actually living that way? Sadly, we estimate that only about 10 percent of the teenaged Christians that we encounter in our ministry are free to live productive lives, lives in which they are able to hear God's voice and obey His great command to make disciples. Spiritual life and freedom are the birthright of every child of God. We've found that those who understand who they are in Christ, and have broken down the false identity equations of the world, are more likely to bear fruit. When we've resolved our spiritual conflicts and claim our freedom in Christ, then our time with God in His Word and our personal prayer lives come alive. Problems and challenges in life don't just disappear, but they can be resolved as we submit to God's Word and submit to the Holy Spirit's leading. There is a big difference between the issues that make up freedom and those that make up growth. There is no such thing as instant maturity. It takes a long time to renew our minds and to be conformed to the image of God. We will certainly never be able to claim perfection in our short lives, but we are not called to model perfection but rather growth. Each day we should strive to become a little more like Jesus.

It is a sure thing that if we are not experiencing true freedom in Christ, there is no way that we can truly experience any kind of significant growth. Without freedom, the steps to maturity become too difficult to climb. Students who have gained an understanding of what

Christ has done for them and have heard God's voice and responded by resolving their personal and spiritual conflicts are free to grow and mature because there are no roadblocks that can't be overcome by submitting to God.

A student stopped by my (Neil's) office one day and said she was researching satanism and wanted to ask me some questions. After talking with her for a few minutes, I suggested that she probably shouldn't be studying that subject.

"Why not?" she asked.

"Because you aren't living a free life in Christ yourself," I responded.

"What do you mean by that?" she asked.

I told her, "You are probably struggling in your Bible classes just trying to pay attention. I suspect that your devotional and prayer life is virtually nonexistent. I would guess that your self-esteem is probably down in the mud somewhere, and you probably entertain a lot of thoughts about suicide."

She almost came out of her chair.

"How did you know that?" she asked.

After years of helping young people find their freedom in Christ, I can frequently discern whether a person is living free in Christ. This same student later took my class that covered the material in our books *Stomping Out the Darkness* and *The Bondage Breaker*. After the class, and with no further counseling, she wrote me this letter:

What I have discovered this last week is this feeling of control. Like my mind is my own. I haven't sat and had these strung out periods of thought and contemplation; that is, conversations with myself. My mind just simply feels quieted. It is really a strange feeling.

My emotions have been stable. I haven't felt depressed once this week. My will is mine. I feel like I have been able to choose to live my life abiding in Christ. Scripture seems different. I have a totally different perspective. I actually understand what it is saying. I feel left alone. Not in a bad way. I'm not lonely, just a single person. For the first time in my life, I believe I actually understand what it means to be a Christian, know who Christ is, and who I am in Him.

I've already had an idea to develop a Bible study from your material and use it next year on my floor for a Bible study. I feel capable of helping people and capable of handling myself. I've been a codependent for years, but this last week I haven't had the slightest need for someone else.

I guess I am describing what it is like to be at peace. I feel this quiet, soft joy in my heart. I have been more friendly with strangers and comfortable. There hasn't been this struggle to get through the day. And then there is the fact that I have been participating actively in life and not passively, critically watching it. Thank you for lending me your hope. I believe I have my own now in Christ.

Do you feel like you are just muddling through life? Are you experiencing the victory and freedom that you have in Christ? If you feel like you are simply muddling, ask God to speak to you in a special way today, to show you who you are in Christ, so you can begin to walk free. If you feel like things are going great, be sure to take time to thank God for His gift of freedom.

Discussion

- Are we supposed to muddle through life with little hope, or is there hope for our freedom? Explain.
- Why are so many people struggling and not walking in freedom?
- Being alive and free in Christ is whose birthright?
- Could you relate to the student who stopped by Neil's office? Explain.
- What did she learn that made such a difference in her life?

The Lie to Reject

I reject the lie that I can find freedom in anyone or anything other than Christ.

The Truth to Accept

I accept the truth that I am free in Christ because I have accepted Jesus as my Savior.

Prayer

Dear heavenly Father, thank You for the freedom You have given me in Christ. Lord, I know I am being transformed into Your likeness and that one day I will be like You. Help me, Father, to not hinder Your work in my life. I want to turn only to You for strength. I pray this in Jesus' name. Amen.

Reading

1 Corinthians 8

Making the Right Choice

*Sin shall not be your master, because you are not
under law, but under grace.*
Romans 6:14

No one likes a lot of rules and regulations. But most of the time, rules and instructions are there for our own protection. I (Dave) love to ski and have taught my three children how to ski. Skiing is a lot of fun if you follow a few simple guidelines. It can be dangerous if you don't!

We used to live a few hours away from Aspen, Colorado, one of the world's best ski areas. People come from all over the world to ski there including the Kennedys. The Kennedy family is known for its daredevil antics and backyard football games. While in Aspen they decided to combine the two sports of skiing and football. They were repeatedly warned by the ski patrol that their football game on skis was not allowed, but they didn't care. After all, they are the Kennedys—powerful, rich, adventurous. No one could tell them what to do. But the rules were not there to spoil their fun; they were there to protect them. Sadly, the Kennedys learned that lesson too late. Michael Kennedy was going out for a pass when he lost control and ran headfirst into a tree. At first, laughter broke out at the awesome wipeout, but the laughter soon turned to fear when he didn't get up right away. Michael never did get up.

This tragic story illustrates what sin is like. It looks fun and harmless. You see it and want to get out there and have fun. So you ignore the warning signs and jump right in. But what looks harmless can also be deadly.

Paul says, "Sin shall not be your master, because you are not under law, but under grace" (Romans 6:14). God has given each of us a free will—the ability to choose right from wrong. So if we wanted to, we could choose to put ourselves back under the law and give up the freedom that Christ gave us through His work on the cross. We can also choose to give in to every sinful desire and embrace a lifestyle of sinful license. Listen to what Paul says about that in Galatians 5:13: "You, my brothers, were called to be free. But do not use your freedom to indulge the sinful nature [flesh]; rather, serve one another in love."

If you choose either extreme, legalism or license, you will realize that each is a dead-end street. At the end of each path is bondage and despair. Fortunately, we have a God who loves us so much that He shows us how to escape those dead-end routes. He also spells out for us how we can repent and have the faith we need to find freedom.

A lot of students today seem to be caught between two terrible groups that are seeking their undivided attention and control. One crowd boasts of its freedom, albeit counterfeit. They have no regard for rules and regulations. Drinking laws to them are out of date and old fashioned. This group doesn't really have a new outlook. It was the same message of the '60s with its free sex and drugs. But that generation learned the staggering consequences of license. Their disregard for any restrictions in their lives was supposed to give them sexual freedom and freedom of expression. Instead it tore up homes and marriages. Sexually transmitted diseases and drug addictions ripped through the very fabric that held their lives together.

The other group uses its good deeds like a sledgehammer to smash anyone who doesn't conform to its rigid code and restrictive lifestyle. You must dress a certain way and conform to the crowd like some manufactured clone that has no individual creativity or freedom to express itself in any way except what is dictated to it by the manipulative group. Oh, how the enemy loves a legalist. They are so easy to talk to. They never measure up. They never truly conform. They are a disappointment to everyone, and they only need to be reminded of how much they fail.

Both groups are active in your world and begging you to join them. Satan doesn't care which group you join, as long as you enlist soon so that he can begin his work of temptation and accusation. As soon as you enlist, his never-ending propaganda will parade through your mind. His goal is not to discourage you but to leave you in complete defeat. His agenda is to kill, steal and destroy.

We believe that there is another small but important third group: those who say no to either legalism or license—to choose the sanctuary of freedom that Christ offers as we follow Him. He offers true safety and security, and He guides us into real freedom: "Now the Lord is the Spirit, and where the Spirit of the Lord is, there is freedom" (2 Corinthians 3:17).

Paul wrote, "All who rely on observing the law are under a curse, for it is written: 'Cursed is everyone who does not continue to do everything written in the Book of the Law.' Clearly no one is justified before God by the law, because, 'The righteous will live by faith'" (Galatians 3:10-11).

The Bible makes it pretty clear that we shouldn't join that legalistic group. After 2,000 years it is amazing how many still choose to join and campaign for that old legalistic group.

Choosing to relate to God on the basis of the law isn't just bad, the Bible says it is actually a curse. I suppose there is a little of the perfectionist in all of us. We all want to do our best; but when our best isn't good enough, we should still be content with who we are and how God has made us. After all, we are still human. The legalist can never accept that. If someone chooses the law, he or she needs to understand just how rigid its standards are. No one can live up to them. James 2:10 says, "Whoever keeps the whole law and yet stumbles at just one point is guilty of breaking all of it." Paul also said of the law, "If a law had been given that could impart life, then righteousness would certainly have come by the law" (Galatians 3:21). But the law is powerless to give life.

Those in the legalistic group believe that simply telling others the law will give them the power to live like Christ. But telling people what they are doing wrong doesn't empower them or give them the strength they need to stop doing it. Salvation doesn't come through our behavior but through our belief in Christ. If salvation had to come through our actions, nobody would qualify for heaven. We would have no hope. No, salvation has come through Christ's sacrifice. Jesus is the life giver. It is His life that gives us the strength to live for Christ and not the law.

Listen to what else the book of Romans has to say about that legalistic group we have been talking about. Romans 7:5 says: "When we were controlled by the sinful nature, the sinful passions aroused by the law were at work in our bodies, so that we bore fruit for death." Paul is saying that rules and regulations (the law) actually stimulate our desire to do what is evil. When we find out something isn't allowed, we naturally seem to want to do it. Paul goes on to say, "But sin, seizing the opportunity afforded by the commandment, produced in me every kind of covetous desire" (Romans 7:8).

If you don't think that is true, remember back to when you were a little kid at Christmastime and you saw your mom and dad come in with their shopping bags filled to the brim. Then, you were instantly exiled to your room. Then about 15 minutes later an announcement was made that you were not under any circumstances to open the hall closet. Now, to be honest, before that moment, you had no real interest in the hall closet. In fact, you never even hung your coat there, even though you were supposed to. But now that the law has been laid down, "Thou shalt not open the hall closet," what do you want to do? As the days crawl by and you get closer and closer to Christmas morning, all you can think about is what's in that closet. The law will always have that same affect: Forbidden fruit will always seem more desirable.

What group are you in today? I think it is pretty obvious what group Jesus would join, and you know you are called to follow Him. It might be hard, but if you need to, consciously choose to avoid legalism and license and follow Him today.

Discussion

· What did you learn from the tragic story about Michael Kennedy? Can you think of others you know who have ignored God's protection, broken the rules and got hurt?
· What is legalism and why is it so dangerous?
· Why do people struggle so much with legalism?
· What is license? Why is it so dangerous?
· Why do people struggle so much with license?

The Lie to Reject

I reject the lie that I am saved because of my good deeds and sacrifices.

The Truth to Accept

I accept the truth that I am saved by who I believe in.

Prayer

Dear heavenly Father, Your follower Paul said that sin shouldn't be my master because I am under grace. Lord, I desire to walk in the freedom that Christ purchased for me. It's so easy to choose to live as though I were still under the law, but that robs me of the freedom I have in Christ. Please reveal to me anything that is keeping me in bondage. I choose to walk free in You today. I pray this in Jesus' name. Amen.

Reading

1 Corinthians 9:1-14

What *Is* God's Law?

*Do not think that I have come to abolish
the Law or the Prophets; I have not come to
abolish them, but to fulfill them.*
Matthew 5:17

Today let's focus on the role that God's law plays in our lives. In life, we are blind to God's ways. We don't naturally know what is right and wrong apart from God. Just like the man in today's story, we need a guide who will direct us in life. As you read, be sure you catch how the man was able to score.

The eyes of college basketball player George Glamack were so bad that he couldn't see the rim of the basket. To him, the backboard was only a dim blur.

Yet, incredibly, Glamack became one of the top scorers in the history of the University of North Carolina. He also earned All-American and the school's College Player of the Year honors in 1940 and 1941.

Because of his poor eyesight and his amazingly accurate hook shots, George was dubbed "The Blind Bomber," a nickname he wore proudly. In fact, the worse Glamack saw, the better he shot.

As a child George suffered from poor eyesight. Despite his vision problems, George turned into a fine young athlete. But at the age of fourteen, Glamack was half blinded from a football injury. George could not see clearly past a few feet.

Basketball was his first love. But when Glamack tried playing again after his eye healed, he couldn't see the basket and could barely make out the backboard. He lost confidence in his ability to shoot, and instead of becoming a starter on the high school team, he wound up on the bench.

George prayed every night for help in regaining his confidence. One day during a high school game, Glamack was sent in for mop-up duty in the last minute. A teammate passed the ball to George. On a lark, George tried a hook shot from fifteen feet away even though he couldn't see the basket. Incredibly, his blind shot swished though the hoop! To George, his prayers had been answered. He knew then and there that despite his poor eyesight, he would one day be a basketball star.

When he graduated, George had grown to six feet, six inches and weighed two hundred pounds and was recruited by the Tar Heels of North Carolina. He turned into a high-scoring starter by his junior year with the help of teammate Bob Rose, a forward with exceptional passing abilities. The two used whistles to communicate. Whenever George heard a certain whistle, he would get in position at a certain spot on the court and wait for a pass from Rose. True to form, the Blind Bomber would turn his back to the basket and score with one of his sweeping hook shoots.

Today, hanging in North Carolina's Smith Center Arena, his number twenty has been an inspiration to other great Tar Heel hoop stars such as Michael Jordan, James Worthy and Bobby Jones.[14]

In the same way that George was able to get in the right place to score because of the signals from Bob, God's law gets us to the place where we can succeed. Bob's signals didn't try to confine and restrict George's play—he was simply placing George where he had the best opportunity to score. In the same way, God did not give us His law to try to confine us and restrict us from having fun in life but rather to set us up in life for the greatest opportunities for success.

Now that we have accepted Christ, we are no longer technically under the Law. Jesus did not come to abolish the Law but to fulfill it. It is important that we understand how to relate to the law. What is God's law anyway? The law is often associated with the commands of the Old Testament. But the concept of God's law is even broader than that. Have you ever heard the word *Torah*? It is the Hebrew word that refers to God's law. It's related to the Hebrew verb *Horah* meaning "to direct or to teach."[15] Just like George was directed to a certain spot on the basketball court, today Christians look to the Torah to direct, teach and instruct us how to live more like Christ. In the New Testament the meaning of the law is not command but rather instruction.

God gave His law as an expression of His will. His instructions, or commands, stem from His holy character. When we study God's law and write it on our hearts as it says to do in God's Word, we are coming in contact with God and His ways (see Isaiah 51:7).

God's law also reveals to us the moral structure of the whole universe. God's moral law is not designed to bring punishment but for the good of all of His creatures. It is God's revelation that brings design and order to His people. This order is a blessing because the moral law protects us from the dangers of sin and the entrapments of bondage. His moral commandments are not primarily restrictive; rather, they are protective and have our best interests at heart—just like the ski patrol who warned Michael Kennedy not to play football on skis (see Day 14). They didn't post the signs and make rules just to ruin his fun. They wanted to protect him from unnecessary dangers. In the same way God's revelation brings true life, peace, well-being and fullness of joy. God's moral laws are designed for the blessing of His people.

Paul describes the Mosaic Law (or the Law of Moses) as "the embodiment of knowledge and truth" (Romans 2:20). The psalmist delighted in God's law, declaring, "Your law is true" (Psalm 119:142). The instructions of the Bible are part of the truth that sanctifies us and sets us apart to follow God's ways rather than the ways of the world. It is part of the truth that brings life as opposed to the lies and deception that lead to suffering and death. The law is an expression of God's holy love for us. We're told to hide God's commands in our hearts and teach them to others (see Deuteronomy 6:6-9).

When we hide God's law in our hearts, it causes us to love God and our neighbor. This love is what God is after. "Love is the fulfillment of the law" (Romans 13:10); "the entire law is summed up in a single command: 'Love your neighbor as yourself'" (Galatians 5:14). So God's law plays an important role in transforming our lives to be more like Christ's life.

What is Christ's relationship to the law? The Bible says that the law has reached its fulfillment in Christ, meaning that God's righteous principles for life are fully realized in Christ. Christ not only fulfilled the law but also terminated all of the law's demand (see Romans 10:4). Christ as the fulfillment of the law is also its goal; that is, the law looked forward to Him. Christ also brought an end to the time when God's people lived under the law like children under a tutor (see Galatians 3:24).

As believers in Christ, Scripture describes us as no longer living under law but being free from the law (see Romans 6:14-15; 7:6). These descriptions of the believer and the law do not mean that we no longer have any relationship to God's law. They do, however, describe a freedom from the law that is absolutely vital to understand for living and growing as God intends.

How do you feel about God's law when you consider that it really is there to protect you and make you more like Christ? Did today's study change your view of the law in any way? I hope that today you will have a greater desire to hide God's Word deep in your heart.

Discussion

- To encounter God's law is to come in contact with what?
- What are the two main points of the law?
- What is Christ's relationship to the law?

The Lie to Reject

I reject the lie that I can fulfill God's law on my own or that the law saves me.

The Truth to Accept

I accept the truth that Christ fulfilled the law and that He is the only means of salvation.

Prayer

Dear heavenly Father, Your law is seen in all of Your dealings with Your people. Your law truly is the embodiment of knowledge and truth. Lord, I agree with the psalmist and declare that Your law is true. Lord, help me better understand You and Your ways so that I can be more like You and others will see Christ in me. I pray this in Jesus' name. Amen.

Reading

1 Corinthians 9:15-27

Free from Bondage

*Christ redeemed us from the curse of the law
by becoming a curse for us.*
Galatians 3:13

In Christ we are free from the law in two significant ways. First, we are free from the legal bondage of the law. Under the law, violators are rightly deserving of punishment. Because everyone has broken the law, we all face the judgment of death. In Christ we are viewed as having died to the law through His sacrificial death for us and are thus released from the Law (see Romans 7:6). "Christ redeemed us from the curse of the law by becoming a curse for us" (Galatians 3:13). As believers in Christ, we have fully met the requirements of the Law in terms of our lawbreaking because we have been identified with Christ in His death (see Romans 6:5).

That's not all! Because we have been identified with Christ's resurrection, we stand in His righteousness—His perfect obedience—so that the law can no longer condemn us in the future. We have become the righteousness of God in Christ; He is our righteousness (see 1 Corinthians 1:30). That's why Paul could say "There is now no condemnation [punishment] for those who are in Christ Jesus, because through Christ Jesus the law of the Spirit of life set me free from the law of sin and death" (Romans 8:1-2). In Christ we are totally free from living under the law as a legal principle in which we either keep the law or pay the penalty. We are now alive in Christ, in whom this principle has been fully fulfilled by His life and death on our behalf.

Not only are we, as believers in Christ, free from the law as a legal requirement, but we are also free from the law as a supervisory custodian of our lives. Paul wrote, "The Law has become our tutor to lead us to Christ, so that we may be justified by faith. But now that faith has come, we are no longer under a tutor" (Galatians 3:24-25, *NASB*). The word "tutor," which suggests a teaching function, is perhaps not the best translation of the Greek word Paul used—*paidagogos*. A paidagogos was usually a slave who was "charged with the supervision and conduct of one or more sons" in the household. He did no formal teaching. His supervision and discipline, of course, did contribute indirectly to the instruction.[16]

Paul's point in using the Greek word "paidagogos" is that the law served this supervisory control over God's people for a limited time—only until Christ came. Paul goes on to explain this truth in Galatians 4:1-5:

What I am saying is that as long as the heir is a child, . . . he is subject to guardians and trustees until the time set by his father. So also, when we were children, we were in slavery under the basic principles of the world. But when the time had fully come, God sent his Son, born of a woman, born under law, to redeem those under law, that we might receive the full rights of sons.

Prior to Christ's coming, God's people were like children under a tutor. But with Christ's work on the cross completed and the sending of the Holy Spirit, believers are now adults and are no longer under the tutor of the law. Although most families do not have a slave performing the function of the paidagogos, our experience of growing up from childhood into adulthood is very illustrative of Paul's words about the change in our relationship to the law.

Since you're not on your own yet, your parents set down rules under which you must live. Those rules have positive effects when you obey, but discipline is applied when you disobey. Eventually, you change your relationship to your parents' rules. You no longer live directly under their laws with the attached rewards and penalties. It is hoped that by that time, the principles of right living, established by your parents' rules, have been instilled in your own mind and heart. You will still relate to your parents' principles, but they will control your life from within instead of from the outside through parental laws.

That is exactly what Paul is talking about in Galatians 4:1-5. Through the finished work of Christ, we have become adult sons and daughters of God. The Holy Spirit has come to dwell in our hearts and effect the new covenant relationship with the law—a relationship described by the prophet Jeremiah: "I will put my law in their minds and write it on their hearts declares the Lord" (Jeremiah 31:33). The change in our relationship to the law does not mean that the law has changed—the moral nature of God has not changed. Rather, the law is no longer an external code written on clay tablets as in the Old Testament. The law is now written on our hearts—the very fountain of our lives—by the presence of the Spirit, who works from our hearts to live it out in our lives.

It is really important to clarify that the Mosaic Law was not a way to earn God's grace. It was not given to the Israelites so that they could become "God's people." God had already, by pure grace, redeemed the people of Israel from the bondage of Egypt when He gave them the Law (see Exodus 19; 20). The believer under the Mosaic Law was thus related to God by faith through God's gracious redemption, even as we are in the New Testament through Christ. The law was never designed to serve as the basis for being rightly related to God.

In the Law, God was simply asking His people to live in accordance with the principles of righteousness that would bring to them the experience of the promised blessing. He graciously provided the sacrificial system by which they could receive forgiveness for their failures and maintain their relationship with Him. He even provided a certain measure of His power to them through the Holy Spirit. But the record of the people under the Old Covenant is that none could ever keep the Law. Sin and sacrifice, over and over again, was their experience—to the point of God's declaration, "You have burdened me with your sins and wearied me with your offenses" (Isaiah 43:24).

Scripture says that under the Old Covenant, the people could never be perfected. The believers living under the Law could never have final peace in relation to sins.

> The old plan was only a hint of the good things in the new plan. Since that old "law plan" wasn't complete in itself, it couldn't complete those who followed it. No matter how many sacrifices were offered year after year, they never added up to a complete solution. If they had, the worshipers would have gone merrily on their way, no longer dragged down by their sins. But instead of removing awareness of sin, when those animal sacrifices were repeated over and over they actually heightened awareness and guilt. The plain fact is that bull and goat blood can't get rid of sin (Hebrews 10:1-4, *THE MESSAGE*).

In that situation, the saints could only look forward to God's final redemption: "O Israel, put your hope in the Lord, for with the Lord is unfailing love and with him is full redemption. He himself will redeem Israel from all their sins" (Psalm 130:7). They looked forward to the day when God would "tread our sins underfoot and hurl all our iniquities into the depths of the sea" (Micah 7:19). They recognized that sin was a power that only God could subdue.

Before Christ, God's people were held under the bondage of the law. They lived their lives under the obligation of the law as a contract with God. But they could never fulfill the contract in perfect righteousness. It stood over them as a supervisory custodian that constantly held them in bondage to the rules and regulations, and the accompanying rewards and punishments.

But believers in Christ are no longer under contract to obey the Law because Christ fulfilled that contract perfectly. Paul said that Christ was born under Law (see Galatians 4:4), meaning that He took upon Himself the full requirements of the Law. He took on not only the punishment that was due for our sin (see Galatians 3:13) but also the obligations that regulate our lives. In His perfect life, He fulfilled all of the righteous commands of the Law.

Every born-again child of God is identified with Christ in His death and resurrection. Therefore the price that the Law demands for our sin has been fully paid. Our new life in Christ is no longer a life controlled by laws and regulations that we could not live up to on our own. We are now alive in Christ and live by the power of the Holy Spirit: "By dying to what once bound us, we have been released from the law so that we serve in the new way of the Spirit, and not in the old way of the written code" (Romans 7:6).

The believer in Christ bears the same relationship to the law that Christ does. Christ, as the end or goal of the law, has fulfilled the law by satisfying its demands both negatively (paying the penalty) and positively (with perfect righteousness). Because the believer is in Christ, these two directions are complete. The believer is free from *all* condemnation and clothed with Christ's righteousness. On our own we cannot meet the righteous demands of the law. Rather, we accept by faith Christ's righteousness to be worked out in our lives so that we might be conformed to the image of our Savior: "For we are God's workmanship, created in Christ Jesus to do good works, which God prepared in advance for us to do" (Ephesians 2:10).

Discussion

- In Christ we are free from the law in what two significant ways?
- What does being an "adult" believer mean?
- Now you relate to your parents' principles, as they enforce them. Soon they will control your life from where?
- The law is not a way to earn what? Why?
- Every born-again child of God is identified with Christ in His death and resurrection. What price do we have to pay for our sin?

The Lie to Reject

I reject the lie that I can earn God's grace by keeping the law.

The Truth to Accept

I accept the truth that I am a born-again child of God and that the price the law demands for my sin has been fully paid by Christ.

Prayer

Dear heavenly Father, thank You that I am Your workmanship, created in Christ Jesus to do good works. I know that You have prepared me to do great things in Your kingdom. I ask for Your strength and leading that I might follow Your will. I pray this in Jesus' name. Amen.

Reading

1 Corinthians 10:1-13

We Are
Responsible

All Scripture is God-breathed and is useful for
teaching, rebuking, correcting and training in righteousness,
so that the man of God may be thoroughly
equipped for every good work.
2 Timothy 3:16-17

It's true that because of our relationship with Christ we are free from any condemnation that the law might bring. Sometimes Christians have expressed a bad attitude toward the law. Our freedom from the law doesn't mean that we as believers are against God's law. As we have said before, our freedom is not a license to sin but rather power to help us live out the life of Christ in our everyday lives. Sometimes God is more concerned about our attitudes than our mere compliance. This next story communicates how important it is to have the right attitude.

My father gave me a great example of self-control when I was a boy watching a church-league softball game.

Dad was forty-three at the time and very active. Though he wasn't known for hitting grand slams, he was good at placing the ball and beating the throw. Singles and doubles were his specialty, and he did the best he could with what he had.

This particular dusty, hot Phoenix evening, Dad poked a good one right over the second baseman's head, and the center fielder flubbed the snag and let the ball bloop between his legs.

My dad saw this as he rounded first base, so he poured on the steam. He was five feet ten inches, 160 pounds, and very fast. He figured that if he sprinted for third and slid, he could beat the throw.

Everyone was cheering as he sent two of his teammates over home plate. The center fielder finally got his feet under him and his fingers around the ball as Dad headed toward third. The throw came as hard and fast as the outfielder could fire it, and Dad started a long slide on that sun-baked infield. Dust flew everywhere.

The ball slammed into the third baseman's glove but on the other side of Dad—the outfield side—away from a clear view by the ump who was still at home plate. Our team's dugout was on the third base side of the diamond, and every one of the players had a clear view of the play.

Dad's foot slammed into third base a solid second before the ball arrived and before the third baseman tagged his leg. But much to the amazement—and then dismay—and then anger—of the team, the umpire, who hesitated slightly before making his call, yelled, "Yerr out!"

Instantly, every member of Dad's team poured onto the field and started shouting at once—Dad's teammates were intent on only one purpose. They wanted to win, and by golly they knew they were right!

The two runners who had crossed home plate before Dad was called out had brought the score within one. If Dad was out—and we all knew he wasn't—his team was robbed of a single run.

With only one inning left, this one bad call could cost them the game.

But just as the fracas threatened to boil over into a mini-riot, Dad silenced the crowd. As the dust settled around him, he held up a hand. "Guys, stop!" he yelled. And then more gently, "There's more at stake here than being right. There's something more important here than winning a game. If the ump says I'm out, I'm out."

And with that, he dusted himself off, limped to the bench to get his glove (his leg was bruised from the slide), and walked back into left field all by himself, ready to begin the last inning. One by one, the guys on his team gave up the argument, picked up their own gloves, and walked out to their positions on the field.

I've got to tell you, I was both bewildered and proud that night. My dad's character was showing, and it sparkled. He may have been dusty, but I saw a diamond standing out there under the lights, a diamond more valuable than all the points his team might have scored.

For a few minutes that evening I was a rich kid, basking in my father's decision to be a man, to hold his tongue instead of wagging it, to settle dust instead of settling a score. I knew his character at that selfless moment was worth more than all the gold-toned plastic trophies you could buy.

Dad held court that night and the verdict came down hard and he was convicted of being a man . . . and the evidence that proved it was his powerful use of that awe-inspiring weapon. Self-control![17]

Oftentimes we expect those who don't know Christ to keep God's law. But trying to keep God's commands before we came to Christ as Savior was unnatural because we "were dead in [our] trespasses and sins . . . and were by nature children of wrath" (Ephesians 2:1-3, *NASB*). People simply can't do it alone because they don't possess God's Holy Spirit to empower them to live a supernatural life. God desires that we walk according to His character and spiritual laws. There is no way we will continue to grow in our sanctification and holiness unless we conform to God's laws. To conform to God's laws is to conform to His character. In other words, we are becoming more like Jesus when our attitudes and actions are more in sync with God's law. God's desire and call for our lives is for our minds to understand His law, our emotions to love His ways and our wills to live out His truths. When we do this, those around us will see the same patterns of holiness that they saw in Jesus, and they will recognize God's work in our lives.

Jesus understood the role that the law was to play in our lives. He never told His followers that they were under the "yoke of the law" or the Old Testament law. Instead, Jesus invited them to "Take my yoke upon you and learn from me" (Matthew 11:29). The law for followers of Christ is no longer the law of Moses but Christ's law, which is described by James as the perfect law and the royal law (see James 1:25; 2:8).

As believers, our ability to keep God's law is a result of our relationship with Jesus. Because we now possess the Holy Spirit, we can fulfill Christ's law with the power of God that is at work in us. We can keep the law because we are children of God. We don't keep the law to become His children; but rather because we are His children, we can keep the law. Rules without a relationship of love will almost always lead to rebellion. Because we are rightly related to God through Christ, it's our heart's desire to obey His law and do His will because of our love for Him. This means that our ability to keep the law comes from our position in Christ. Our sanctification is working itself out in the righteousness that is ours because we are children of God and we've been placed in Christ.

We cannot sanctify ourselves simply by keeping the law. Remember, it is not *what we do* that determines who we are; it is *who we are* that determines what we do. Sanctification is applying the finished work of Christ in our lives through the power of the Holy Spirit. We stand against the unrighteousness of this world by clothing ourselves with Christ (see Romans 13:14; Galatians 3:27).

The Holy Spirit gives us the power we need to overcome any sin and bondage in our lives and helps us display the character of Christ in our everyday lives. "Live by the Spirit," Paul said, "and you will not gratify the desires of the sinful nature" (Galatians 5:16). We can meet the righteous requirements of the law by living according to the Spirit (see Romans 8:4). And against the fruit of the Spirit—love, joy, peace, kindness, goodness, faithfulness, gentleness and self-control—there is no law (see Galatians 5:22-23). One thing that we can't overemphasize is that our ability to obey and live out Christ's law comes only through the power of the Holy Spirit and not from our own willpower. No amount of desire on the part of our flesh can manifest the fruit of the Spirit. Only as we submit to the Spirit's power can we live a life that is victorious and become obedient to God's law.

Remember: God isn't interested in perfection; He's concerned about growth. Do you have an attitude that desires growth?

Discussion

- Are Christians against the law? Explain.
- The grace of God is not a license to sin. It is a power that enables us to what?
- Why is it unnatural to try to keep the law before coming to Christ?
- What is the law for Christians? What does this mean?
- The power to overcome sin and live out the righteousness of Christ's law comes from whom?

The Lie to Reject

I reject the lie that I can keep Christ's law apart from my position in Christ.

The Truth to Accept

I accept the truth that it's not what I do that determines who I am; rather, it is who I am in Christ that determines what I do.

Prayer

Dear heavenly Father, I know it is not what I do that determines who I am. It is who I am that determines what I do. My identity is not found in the law or in my ability to keep the law. I know that the only way I am declared righteous is through Christ's sacrifice on the cross. I choose to find my significance and security in Christ and not in my ability to keep the law. I pray this in Jesus' name. Amen.

Reading

1 Corinthians 10:14-22

He First Loved Us

God so loved the world that he gave his one and only Son, that whoever believes in him shall not perish but have eternal life.

John 3:16

If you were invited to go to a prison and had the opportunity to share truths from the Bible with a handful of the worst criminals in the world but only had 10 minutes to share, what would you say? The most important point to convey would be the great love that God has for each and every one of them. John 3:16, today's verse, gives us some idea of the extent of that love.

Understanding God's love for us is the only thing that can awaken hope in our lives, and it's the most powerful motivation for living, even if we're not behind bars. Prison, and this world for that matter, can be a fearful place. But Christ's love and His sacrifice for us overcome our fears, especially the fear of eternal punishment. We know we've sinned and deserve punishment, but His loving sacrifice provides forgiveness and hope that destroys our fears. "There is no fear in love. But perfect love drives out fear, because fear has to do with punishment. The one who fears is not made perfect in love" (1 John 4:18).

Satan and the world like to motivate people through fear. Sometimes, sadly, misguided Christians will lay down the law without the gospel's message of grace. They flatly deny the power of God's love and grace that is evidenced in the gospel. Love was the greatest motivation that Jesus used in the New Testament to inspire His followers. Because Jesus completely fulfilled the law in every way on our behalf, the law doesn't motivate us. Instead, we are motivated by God's love and our adoption into the family of God. It was Jesus' great sacrifice on the cross and His resurrection that have allowed us to become new creatures in Christ.

During the peak of the war in what was formerly Yugoslavia, I (Neil) was training Croatian pastors in a Christian refugee center. Listening in was a Bosnian refugee named Mohammed who had been raised in the Islamic tradition, with all its fatalistic legalism. After listening to me teach for four days about the gracious love of God and how we could be free in Christ, he asked through an interpreter to see me. That night I had the privilege of leading him to Christ. He asked to be baptized, and the next day he was baptized in the Adriatic Sea.

Mohammed had arrived at the refugee center just a week earlier with his two daughters, who appeared to be deaf, either from physical injury or psychological scars. They had seen their mother blown up before their eyes by a mortar attack. They also had always been told that Christians were their enemy. The day after their father was baptized, these two innocent little girls—ravaged by the war—said with wonder in their eyes, "Jesus loves me!" I will never hear those words uttered again by anyone without realizing the power of that truth to transform lives.

Laying down the law will not set people free; only Christ can do that. Overbearing rule makers leave people in bondage to legalism. If we want to help people find their freedom in Christ, the love of God must compel us.

Shortly after World War II came to a close, Europe began picking up the pieces. Much of the Old Country had been ravaged by war and was in ruins. Perhaps the saddest sight of all was that of little orphaned children starving in the streets of those war-torn cities.

Early one chilly morning an American soldier was making his way back to the barracks in London. As he turned the corner in his jeep, he spotted a little boy with his nose pressed to the window of a pastry shop. Inside, the cook was kneading dough for a fresh batch of doughnuts. The hungry boy stared in silence, with his nose pressed against the window, drooling and watching the cook's every move. The soldier pulled his jeep to the curb, stopped, and got out.

"Son, would you like some of those?"

The boy was startled. "Oh yeah . . . I would."

The American stepped inside and bought a dozen, put them in a bag and walked back to where the lad was standing in the foggy cold of the London morning. He smiled, held out the bag and said simply, "Here you are."

As he turned to walk away, he felt a tug on his coat. He looked back and heard the child ask quietly, "Mister . . . are you God?" When people love people with no strings attached, they are really loving like Jesus.[18]

Love has its source only in God, and it is God's love that enables the believer to love: "We love because he first loved us" (1 John 4:19). It is God's love that moves us to obey the law of Christ. Love is the essence of lawkeeping, as Jesus demonstrated when He washed the feet of His disciples. Then He said "My command is this: Love each other as I have loved you" (John 15:12). Paul said, "The entire law is summed up in a single command: 'Love your neighbor as yourself'" (Galatians 5:14).

But it doesn't stop there. Not only has God given us this incredible outpouring of His love and blessing, but God has also given us guidelines for living. The law was put in place so that we might have a fruitful life filled with God's blessing. The commands of Christ are important ingredients in God's recipe when it comes to making us more like His Son, Jesus. The law transforms us and is used in our sanctification. Do you look at God's commands as restrictions or as tools to guide you into an abundant life? Today, ask the Lord how you can display His love by obeying His will.

Discussion

- Have you ever done something because you were afraid of what would happen if you didn't do it?
- Explain the consequences of teaching the law without grace.
- When has your love for Jesus made you want to obey Him?
- What can you do to be more obedient to Jesus? To your parents?
- What's the best way to motivate people?

The Lie to Reject

I reject the lie that love comes from any source other than God!

The Truth to Accept

I accept the truth that we love because God first loved us.

Prayer

Dear heavenly Father, Your Word says that I love You because You first loved me. Thanks for loving me so much that You paid the penalty for my sin. Help me to understand the great depths of Your love for me. Lord, I don't want fear to control my life, and I know that Your love casts out all fear. Thank You. I pray in Jesus' name. Amen.

Reading

1 Corinthians 10:23-33

Abiding in Christ

*Abide in Me, and I in you. As the branch cannot
bear fruit of itself unless it abides in the vine, so neither can you
unless you abide in Me. I am the vine, you are the branches;
he who abides in Me and I in him, he bears much fruit,
for apart from Me you can do nothing.*
John 15:4-5, *NASB*

Are you content just to learn a few stories and facts about Jesus, or do you want your life to be a reflection of His? If you want to reflect Christ, then you will want to learn how to abide in Christ. Abiding is like getting right next to Jesus and getting to know Him so well that you understand His plans and desires. In your life you begin to care deeply about His concerns, and you make an effort to plan your day's activities to conform around His will. To be honest, abiding isn't presented as an option for believers—it's a necessity. It's impossible for you to live like Jesus and bear fruit apart from Christ. The Bible clearly says that without Christ, you can do nothing. It is only by God's loving grace that you can live a Spirit-filled life. Only when you abide in Christ does God become visible in your life. You can know tons of biblical facts, but if you don't have character, then you're only a noisy gong or clanging symbol that has no love (see 1 Corinthians 13:1).

Not only does abiding help us demonstrate holiness, but it also allows us to get close to God and experience Him intimately. When we are close to Him, we can hear His voice and be built up by His loving encouragement—just like the young girl in this story.

As a teenager, I worked as a waitress at a Coco's restaurant, in Southern California. Although California nights are supposed to be warm, on this particular February night the brisk wind shrieked though the front door. Around nine o'clock things slowed down and that's when I started feeling sorry for myself. You see, all my friends had gone to the movies, but I had to work until closing.

I didn't pay much attention to the man who entered the restaurant. A flurry of leaves followed him in. The sound of the wailing wind fell silent as the door shut itself. I busied my-self making more coffee. Suddenly the hostess grabbed my arm. "This is really creepy," she whispered, "but there is a man with a white moustache over there who said he wouldn't eat here unless you were his waitress."

I swallowed hard. "Is he a weirdo?"

"See for yourself," she said.

We carefully peered through the decorative foliage at the mysterious man in the corner. Slowly he lowered his menu, revealing thick, white hair, silver-blue eyes and a wide grin beneath his white moustache. He lifted his hand and waved.

"That's no weirdo!" I said. "That's my dad."

"You mean he came to see you at work?" The hostess balked. "That's pretty strange, if you ask me." I didn't think it was very strange. I thought it was kind of neat. But I didn't let Dad know that. Poor Dad! I acted so nonchalant, rattling off the soup of the day and scribbling down his order before anyone could see him squeeze my elbow and say, "Thanks, honey." But I want you to know something—I never forgot that night. His being there said a thousand things to me. As he silently watched me clear tables and refill coffee cups, I could hear his unspoken words bouncing off the wall: "I'm here. I support you. I'm proud of you. You're doing a great job. Keep up the good work. You're my girl. I love you." It was the best valentine I received that year.[19]

Just as the dad in the story gave his daughter a special valentine by his presence, Jesus gives us a special message of love every time we come into His presence. That's what abiding is all about.

Abiding is the only way we can continue God's work of progressive sanctification. That supernatural work can only be accomplished if we tap into the presence of God. If we look to ourselves, we'll fail. If we abide in Him, we'll experience Christ's victory. Only God can release us from the chains of sin, set us free from our past and make us children of God. Even though we have been transformed in to new creations and possess a new divine nature, we still must depend on God's abiding presence to supply the strength we need to live in this world and become like Jesus. Being Christians does not mean that we have more power in and of ourselves. It means that we are inwardly connected to the only source of power that is able to overcome the laws of sin and death—that source of power is the law of the Spirit of life in Christ Jesus (see Romans 8:2).

So many things in life draw us away from God. The world, the flesh and the devil are constantly trying to pull us away from our dependence on God and trying to get us to rely on our own feeble human intelligence and resources. No matter how hard we try in the flesh to be like Jesus, we will never be able to live righteously without the Holy Spirit. The power to live the Christian life comes from dependence not self-determination.

As long as we think we can live the Christian life by ourselves, we will fail miserably. Wisdom says, "Trust in the Lord with all your heart and lean not on your own understanding; in all your ways acknowledge him, and he will make your paths straight" (Proverbs 3:5-6).

What does Christian growth look like? Luke 2:52 gives us a glimpse: "Jesus grew in wisdom and stature, and in favor with God and men." Jesus, because He was God, grew up perfectly in every way. There was never a time in His life when He wasn't balanced spiritually, mentally, physically and socially. We are fortunate today to have many wonderful Christian books that help us in many areas of Christian growth. There are books about dating, not dating, purity, prayer and just about every other spiritual discipline. Yet many of these excellent resources fail to help people because if you are not abiding in and connected to Christ, the power source, no principle can be implemented in your life. Take a look at this chart so that we can show you what we mean.

Figure 5

Personal Disciplines

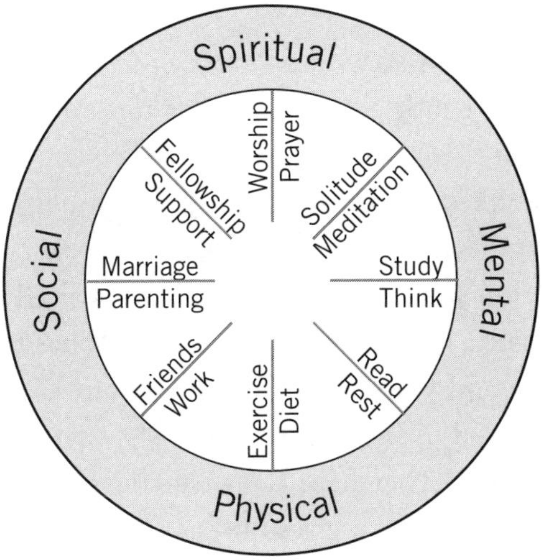

As you look at figure 5, you see the various Christian disciplines. Each activity is like a spoke in a Christian wheel. As you can see, the spokes are pointed toward the hub of the wheel, but they are not connected. In other words, there is no abiding taking place. Without abiding, those Christian disciplines are being done in the flesh. Self-discipline without abiding in Christ is nothing more than Christian behaviorism: "You shouldn't do that; you should do this. That is not the best way to do that; here is a better way to do it." And you dutifully respond, "Okay, I'll try my best." The result is a try-harder lifestyle: "You're not trying hard enough. If only you will try harder, maybe your Christianity will work!" The result? Guilt. Condemnation. Defeat. If you think about it, you probably know someone who has accepted Christ as his or her Savior but is not walking with the Lord. This person has given up living for Christ. You might ask, "Why would he or she do that?" Much of the time, it's because he or she has been living out Christian disciplines through the strength of the flesh rather than abiding in Christ. Instead of responding to a calling in ministry, he or she has probably been driven by some sense of guilt and twisted obligation. It is just a matter of time before anyone would become disillusioned and want to abandon that kind of fruitless pursuit. Sadly, the further one is from the hub of the wheel (see figure 5), the harder he or she will try—until his or her life breaks down.

When we abide in Christ, we aren't just close to the hub—we are connected to it. Christ's gentle and kind desires for our lives naturally flow out of us: We aren't driven we are motivated.

Just as people liked to hang around Jesus, you'll find that as you abide in Christ, people will want to hang around you.

People who reject Jesus' invitation to abide with Him become judgmental and legalistic. They can tell what the Bible has to say about how we should behave and what we should do in our Christian life. They know all the dos and don'ts, but they lack the power to demonstrate the true fruit of the Spirit. They have captured the letter of the law, which kills, but not the Spirit, which gives life (see 2 Corinthians 3:6).

When we fail to abide in Christ, all of our relationships suffer. They eventually become shallow and distant. Anyone who makes an attempt to really get to know us is pushed away because our defensive walls go up due to our insecurity. As a result we withdraw even more. Then we either become very passive or very pushy and controlling. We won't let anyone close for fear that he or she will find out what our life is really like and how much we are struggling. That doesn't sound like freedom in Christ. But God wants us to have relationships through which we can both be encouraged and encourage others to be more like Christ. That only comes as we abide in Christ. How close do you want to be to Jesus today? Don't let your feelings dictate your choices. Even if you don't feel like getting close to Jesus, ask Him to give you the strength to abide in Him.

Discussion

- What does the Bible say about you if you know the principles of the Bible but don't have godly character (see 1 Corinthians 13:1)?
- Becoming a Christian means that we are inwardly connected to the only source of power that can overcome sin and death. Where does this true power come from?
- What should we rely on instead of our own intellect and resources?
- If we fail to abide in Christ, why will our relationships suffer?

The Lie to Reject

I reject the lie that I have the power to live the Christian life on my own.

The Truth to Accept

I accept the truth that only with Christ and His strength can I do all things.

Prayer

Dear heavenly Father, help me to not be judgmental and legalistic. I want to do more than tell people what's right and wrong. I want to truly love others the way You do! I don't want to be like those who have captured the letter of the law; rather,

I want to hold fast to the Spirit who gives life. I want to be one who shares Your wonderful grace, mercy and abundant life. I pray in Jesus' name. Amen.

Reading

1 Corinthians 11:1-16

Where Changed Behavior Begins

For as [a man] thinks in his heart, so is he.
Proverbs 23:7, *NKJV*

Who you are makes a difference. Consider the following story:

A teacher in New York decided to honor each of her seniors in high school by telling them the difference they each made. She called each student to the front of the class, one at a time. First she told them how the student made a difference to her and the class. Then she presented each of them with a blue ribbon with gold letters that read, "Who I Am Makes a Difference."

Afterward the teacher decided to do a class project to see what kind of impact recognition would have on a community. She gave each of the students three more ribbons and instructed them to go out and spread this acknowledgment ceremony. Then they were to follow up on the results, see who honored whom, and report back to the class in about a week.

One of the boys in the class went to a junior executive in a nearby company and honored him for helping him with his career planning. He gave him a blue ribbon and put it on his shirt. Then he gave him two extra ribbons and said, "We're doing a class project on recognition, and we'd like you to go out, find somebody to honor, give them a blue ribbon, then give them the extra blue ribbon so they can acknowledge a third person to keep this acknowledgment ceremony going. Then please report back to me and tell me what happened."

Later that day the junior executive went in to see his boss, who had been noted, by the way, as being kind of a grouchy fellow. He sat his boss down and he told him that he deeply admired him for being a creative genius. The boss seemed very surprised. The junior executive asked him if he would accept the gift of the blue ribbon and would he give him permission to put it on him. His surprised boss said, "Well, sure."

The junior executive took the blue ribbon and placed it right on his boss's jacket above his heart. As he gave him the last extra ribbon, he said, "Would you do me a favor? Would you take this extra ribbon and pass it on by honoring somebody else? The young boy who first gave me the ribbons is doing a project in school and we want to keep this recognition ceremony going and find out how it affects people."

That night the boss came home to his fourteen-year-old son and sat him down. He said, "The most incredible thing happened to me today. I was in my office and one of the junior executives came in and told me he admired me and gave me a blue ribbon for being a creative genius. Imagine. He thinks I'm a creative genius. Then he put this blue ribbon that says 'Who I Am Makes A Difference' on my jacket above my heart. He gave me an extra ribbon and asked me to find somebody else to honor. As I was driving home tonight, I started thinking about whom I would honor with this ribbon and I thought about you. I want to honor you. My days are really hectic and when I come home I don't pay a lot of attention to you. Sometimes I scream at you for not getting enough good grades in school and for your bedroom being a mess, but somehow tonight, I just wanted to sit here and well . . . just let you know that you do make a difference to me. Besides your mother, you are the most important person in my life. You're a great son, and I love you!"

The startled boy started to sob and sob, and he couldn't stop crying. His whole body shook. He looked up at his father and said through his tears, "Dad, I didn't think it mattered to you whether I lived or died. Now I know it does."[20]

Who you are truly does make a difference. In the Bible, the first half of every letter to the churches talks about who we are in Christ. These letters say that we are children of God. This is God's way of pinning a special ribbon on our chests and saying we belong. We are now holy and righteous. We're saints.

Today's key verse reminds us that who we are on the outside is a reflection of who we are on the inside. If we have lies in our belief system, then we will struggle in our behavior. If we want to change, we must first be alive and established in Christ. When we know that we are children of God, then biblical teaching will become effective. We will never display the law of Christ in our lives without first having a deep-rooted understanding of our position in Him. A Christ-centered wheel displaying personal disciplines is represented by figure 6.

We are not saying that there is anything wrong with great programs like witnessing, serving the poor or anything else that helps us change our behavior. We need all the help we can get when it comes to improving our relationships and making our families stronger as long as such programs are Christ centered. We get messed up, however, when we look to the program and not to Christ. Instead of seeking intimacy with God, we want a new technique or another model for ministry. If we look to a program rather than to the person of Christ, we will get burned out, our flesh will get tired, and we will give up.

Figure 6

Personal Christ-Centered Disciplines

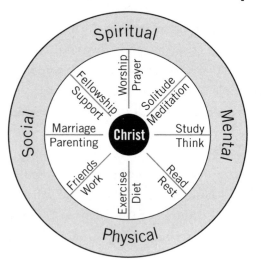

Do you want to truly glorify God? Listen to what Jesus said, "This is to my Father's glory, that you bear much fruit, showing yourselves to be my disciples" (John 15:8). Don't miss the point here. Some read that verse and miss the whole point. They walk away saying, "I have to bear fruit!" But what does verse 5 say? "He who abides in Me and I in him, he bears much fruit" (John 15:5, *NASB*). Bearing fruit is the evidence that we are abiding in Christ. If we are abiding in Christ, then any program will work. If we try to live the Christian life in our own strength, then no program will work. Of course, when we abide in Christ, a good program will bear more fruit than a bad program.

Discussion

- The Bible's practical instructions are found in what part of Paul's epistles?
- Why can't we approach the Christian life merely by looking at the practical applications?
- What is the significance of Proverbs 23:7, *NKJV*: "As [a man] thinks in his heart, so is he" How does this verse relate to our freedom in Christ?

The Lie to Reject

I reject the lie that I can live the Christian life in my own strength and that my program will work.

The Truth to Accept

I accept the truth that if we are abiding in Christ, then any program will work.

Prayer

Dear heavenly Father, I know the only way I can bear real and lasting fruit is to abide in You. Lord, I know that I have trusted in my own strength in the past and looked to programs and methods to make me feel close to You. I turn from those things now and turn to You and choose to abide in You. I pray in Jesus' name. Amen.

Reading

1 Corinthians 11:17-34

God, Our Power Source

It is no longer I who live, but Christ lives in me.
Galatians 2:20, *NASB*

Sanctification—becoming more like Jesus—can only happen when we depend on God. It is only through His Spirit that we have any hope of being sanctified. We are to stay connected to Jesus and close to Him because without Him, we can do nothing (see John 15:4-9).

Our lives, as believers, are to center around the Spirit. That is why the Bible says that we are to walk in the Spirit (see Galatians 5:16, *NASB*). We are to yield ourselves in every way to the Spirit's control so that we are filled to the full (see Ephesians 5:18). So many Christians today are content to let Jesus have only a small percentage of their lives. But Jesus isn't content with 90 or even 99 percent of our lives—He wants 100 percent. Today, we want to talk about that kind of growth and devotion to Christ. What does it mean to abide in Christ and to have the power of the Holy Spirit in your life?

In the Bible verses we just mentioned, we see that Christ, the Holy Spirit and the Father are all involved in our daily growth. Before we talk about what happens in day-by-day sanctification, let's look at the roles that the Father, the Son and the Holy Spirit have in our growth.

Our *salvation* involves the activity of each person of the Trinity—Father, Son and Holy Spirit. Their roles in the saving process are seen in Titus 3:4-6: "When the kindness and love of God our Savior appeared, . . . He saved us through the washing of rebirth and renewal by the Holy Spirit, whom he poured out on us generously through Jesus Christ our Savior."

The love of the Father is the source of salvation; the Holy Spirit applies that salvation to us, and the salvation that the Holy Spirit brings has been made possible by Christ's work and, therefore, comes through Him. This pattern is seen again in Romans 8:2-4. God sent His Son to do what the law could not do (set us free from the law of sin and death) so that the righteousness of the law might be met in those who live according to the Spirit.

Our *sanctification* depends on the work of the entire Godhead, or Trinity. The Father is the fountain of all salvation, but that salvation is worked out by Christ through the Spirit. Scripture places our focus on all three when it talks about sanctification. Christ, by His perfect life and sacrificial death, conquered sin and death. He made it possible for us to become restored to our proper relationship with God and thus to be alive with God's life and righteousness. It is the Spirit's work to bring Christ into us so that His salvation might become operative in our experience.

The Bible frequently mentions that Christ and the Spirit both participate in the work of salvation, especially in relation to our sanctification. We are "sanctified in Christ Jesus" (1 Corinthians 1:2); we are "sanctified by the Holy Spirit" (Romans 15:16). We are to "walk in [Christ Jesus]" (Colossians 2:6, *NASB*); we are to "walk by the Spirit" (Galatians 5:16, *NASB*). We are called "into fellowship with his Son Jesus Christ" (1 Corinthians 1:9); we are blessed with "the fellowship of the Holy Spirit" (2 Corinthians 13:14). We have received the Spirit that "we may understand what God has freely given us," and therefore "we have the mind of Christ" (1 Corinthians 2:12,16). In all these passages, the same reality given to us in Christ through His saving work is applied to us by the Spirit. The Spirit brings into our lives the presence of the risen Lord and all that He is. What Christ does, the Spirit does.

We see this connection again in Christ's letters to the seven churches found in Revelation chapters 2 and 3. Each letter closes with the words: "He who has an ear, let him hear what the Spirit says to the churches" (Revelation 2:7,11,17,29; 3:6,13,22). Notice that the key is not whether Christ will speak to the Church; the key is whether the Church is listening to the Spirit. In the Old Testament, the Spirit came as the Spirit of God, powerfully effecting God's work in the world. He was God at work on Earth. In the same way in the New Testament, the Spirit was sent by Christ and came as the Spirit of Christ (see Romans 8:9; Galatians 4:6; Philippians 1:19). He is the powerful presence of Christ on Earth, doing His saving work in the lives of people.

Paul's prayer for the believers in Ephesus helps us to better understand the relationship between the Spirit and Christ in the Christian life:

> I pray that . . . [the Father] may strengthen you with power through his Spirit in your inner being, so that Christ may dwell in your hearts through faith. And I pray that you . . . may have power, together with all the saints, to grasp how wide and long

and high and deep is the love of Christ, and to know this love . . .
that you may be filled to the measure of all the fullness of God
(Ephesians 3:16-19).

Jesus taught this same truth when He said that the Spirit "will bring
glory to me by taking from what is mine and making it known to you"
(John 16:14). The Spirit works in us to cause us to see Jesus for who He
really is. We confess Christ as Lord only by the Spirit (see 1 Corinthians
12:3). The Spirit not only ministers to us in our initial salvation, but
He also causes us to continue focusing on Christ in faith so that He
becomes more and more at home in our hearts—the center of our per-
sonality, the place where our thoughts, emotions and actions start—"the
wellspring of life" (Proverbs 4:23).

Let's tie this together. The Spirit empowers us to lay hold of Christ,
grasp His incomprehensible love for us and focus on His way of life so
that it might be lived in us. Our walk by the Spirit is one of focusing on
Christ in faith so that we abide in Him and His life is formed in us.

The two basic principles of our growth are to remain focused on
Christ through every means by which He is revealed, and to stay open to
the Spirit of God, who works in us to make Christ's victorious life
dynamic in our lives.

Discussion

- The Bible repeatedly teaches us that sanctification in our daily lives
  is possible only through what?
- What can we accomplish if we fail to abide in Christ?
- What are some of the positive effects of abiding in Christ?
- What does it mean to walk in the Spirit?
- What does walking in the Spirit have to do with our sanctification?

The Lie to Reject

I reject the lie that walking according to the flesh and my own desire will
ever bring true peace.

The Truth to Accept

I accept the truth that walking in the Spirit is the true road to freedom and peace in my life.

Prayer

Dear heavenly Father, I want to keep in step with Your Spirit and walk according to Your Spirit. Help me to hear Your voice and stay in Your Word so that I might better understand Your ways. Lord, I know that the flesh will try to control my walk with You, but I choose to crucify the flesh and do Your will. I pray in Jesus' name. Amen.

Reading

1 Corinthians 12:1-11

Abiding in Christ Daily

As you therefore have received Christ Jesus the Lord, so walk in Him, having been firmly rooted and now being built up in Him and established in your faith, just as you were instructed.
Colossians 2:6-7, *NASB*

Abiding in Christ is something we need to do every day of our lives. By staying connected to Him, we can ensure that we'll continue to grow and become more like Him. We need to remember that He is always with us, watching us and encouraging us when the going gets tough. This next story illustrates the power of a relationship and how a young man was able to achieve at a higher level when he understood someone was watching.

Lou Little was football coach at Georgetown University. The college president came to him one day and, naming a student, said, "Lou, do you know this fellow?"

"Sure," Lou answered, "he's been on my squad four years. I've never played him. He's good enough—he's just not motivated."

"Well," the president continued, "we just heard that his father died. Will you break the news to him?"

The coach put his arm around the boy in a back room, "Take a week off, Son, I'm sorry." It was Tuesday. Friday, Coach Little came into his locker room to see the student back and suiting up. "What are you doing back already?" Little inquired.

"The funeral was yesterday, Coach. So I came back. You see, tomorrow's the big game and I've got to play in it."

"Wait a minute, son," Little said, "you know I've never started you."

"But you will start me tomorrow and you won't be sorry," the moist-eyed boy stated firmly.

Softening, the coach decided that if he won the toss-up he would use the boy on the first play. He couldn't do any damage on the first return. Well, Georgetown won the toss. On the first play this fatherless boy came down the field like a tornado. Coach Little, shocked, left him in for another play. He blocked, he tackled, he passed, he ran. He literally won the ball game that day for Georgetown University.

In the locker room Coach Little, perplexed, asked, "Son, what happened?"

The happy, perspiring victor said, "Coach, you never knew my dad, did you? Well, sir, he was blind and today was the first time he ever saw me play."[21]

We need to remember that our dad is watching over us all the time. When we remember that we are connected to God through Christ, the process of growing up in the Lord goes easier. Check out what God's Word has to say about growing up.

> *Clothe yourselves with the Lord Jesus Christ*, and do not think about how to gratify the desires of the sinful nature (Romans 13:14, emphasis added).

> I no longer live, but Christ lives in me. The life I live in the body, I live by faith *in the Son of God* (Galatians 2:20, emphasis added).

> Be strong *in the Lord* and in his mighty power (Ephesians 6:10, emphasis added).

> We grow by "holding fast to the head," which is Christ (Colossians 2:19, *NASB*).

> Whatever you do, whether in word or deed, *do it all in the name of the Lord Jesus* (Colossians 3:17, emphasis added).

It's pretty obvious in these verses that the ability to live the Christian life is completely tied to our relationship with Christ.

The Bible makes it clear that abiding in Jesus involves two important practices. First, we are to build ourselves up by trusting in all that Jesus has done for us. Second, we are to obey Jesus in every way and do what He says, even when we don't always want to. To put it simply, we are to trust and obey.

Abiding in Christ means I have accepted Jesus' saving work through faith and am allowing His life to be lived through me. Another important part of abiding in Christ on a daily basis is letting His Word dwell in us. "If you abide in Me, and My words abide in you . . ." (John 15:7, *NASB*; see also John 8:31; 1 John 2:24).

When Jesus told us that He abided in His Father, He was making it clear that He had lived a life of complete obedience to God the Father. Not once did Jesus fail to fulfill even the smallest wish of the Father. So it makes sense that if we are to abide in Christ, we too are to live in obedience to our Savior. Since we are to abide in the Word of God, we are naturally expected to study the Bible until its words get lodged in our hearts and our minds, until it affects our actions. If we allow that to happen, we will bear good fruit (see John 15:1-8).

We can't overemphasize the importance of raw obedience on our part to ensure that we are abiding in Christ. Jesus said, "Abide in My love. If you keep My commandments, you will abide in My love; just as I have kept My Father's commandments and abide in His love" (John 15:9-10, *NASB*).

When we live as Jesus lived and try to show the same kind of love He showed, we are truly abiding and keeping one of the greatest commandments. Jesus said, "A new commandment I give to you, that you love one another, even as I have loved you" (John 13:34, *NASB*). "The one who says he abides in Him ought himself to walk in the same manner as He walked" (1 John 2:6, *NASB*).

Being transformed into the image of Jesus isn't a quick process. There are a lot of changes going on inside as you continue to walk and abide in Christ. Don't expect that you will change overnight. Don't get discouraged, but rather remember that Jesus said that His yoke is easy and His load is light (see Matthew 11:30). Also remember that those around you need time to grow up as well. Remember to treat others with the same mercy you would like to receive.

Sometimes we don't realize the terrible hurt and devastation that have occurred in the lives of others. The following is a poem from one girl who experienced terrible abuse as a child. Yet her poem describes the hope and transformation that abiding in Christ brings.

The Wreath

A friend of mine whose grapevine died, had put it out
    for trash.

I said to her, "I'll take that vine and make something of that."
At home the bag of dead, dry vines looked nothing but a mess,
     but as I gently bent one vine, entwining 'round and 'round,
a rustic wreath began to form, potential did abound.
One vine would not go where it should, and anxious as I was,
I forced it so to change its shape, it broke—and what the cause?
     If I had taken precious time to slowly change its form,
It would have made a lovely wreath, not a dead vine, broken,
     torn.
As I finished bending, adding blooms, applying trim, I realized
     how the rustic wreath is like my life within.
You see, so many in my life have tried to make me change.
     They've forced my spirit anxiously, I tried to rearrange.
But when the pain was far too great, they forced my fragile form,
     I plunged far deeper in despair, my spirit broken, torn.
Then God allowed a gentle one that knew of dying vines, to
     kindly, patiently allow the Lord to take His time.
And though the vine has not yet formed a decorative wreath, I
     know that with God's servants' help one day when Christ
     I meet,
He'll see a finished circle, a perfect gift to Him.
It will be a final product, a wreath with all the trim.
So as you look upon this gift, the vine round and complete,
     remember God is using you to gently shape His wreath.[22]

We can grow by focusing on Christ and abiding in Him by faith so that His life is lived in us. Today, we need to ask God to help us abide in Him and conform us a little bit more to the image of our awesome Savior.

Discussion

- Scripture reveals that abiding in Christ involves two basic practices. What are they?
- What does abiding in Christ mean to you?

- Why does abiding in Christ mean more than just thinking about truth?
- How can we personally relate to Jesus as the way, the truth and the life?

The Lie to Reject

I reject the lie that I can change overnight and that God is forcing me to do so.

The Truth to Accept

I accept the truth that conforming to the image of God is a long, steady process of change, but someday I will be like Christ!

Prayer

Almighty God, it's a real temptation for me to stop depending on You, and rely on my own talents and resources to live life. Please keep teaching me how to live by the Spirit's power, how to abide in You and how to walk by faith so that I can grow in holiness. I thank You, God, for the gift of Your Son and the power of Your Spirit so that I can be sanctified and bear fruit for Your kingdom. In Jesus' name, amen.

Reading

1 Corinthians 12:12-31

Filled with the Spirit

*So I say, live by the Spirit, and you will not gratify
the desires of the sinful nature.*
Galatians 5:16

America held its breath at the news that John F. Kennedy, Jr., was missing. His small plane had disappeared off the radar fewer than 10 miles from his destination. John was a new pilot and had only received his pilot's license a year before. He and his wife, Carolyn, and her sister were taking the short trip from New Jersey to Martha's Vineyard to visit friends and attend a family wedding. John had a VFR, or visual flight rating, meaning he was allowed to fly by line of sight only. Only pilots with an IFR, or instrument flight rating, were allowed to fly through clouds. If John encountered cloudy conditions or his visibility was impaired in any way, he would be required to land. John had thought about taking a flight instructor with him because of a leg injury he had received but decided not to at the last minute. That choice may have been a fatal error.

As hours turned to days, fear turned to tears as wreckage from John's plane began to wash ashore. Finally the sad news came that the bodies of all three—John, Carolyn and Lauren—had been found a short distance from Martha's Vineyard. No one knows what caused the terrible crash. Some think he went into a death spiral. This is a condition in which you become disoriented and don't realize you are turning as you descend. Seeing that you're going down rapidly, you pull back on the flight controls, but this only causes you to descend more rapidly into a death spin. We may never know what really happened, but one thing is certain: He needed a guide. If only he had had an instructor with him that night!

Like John, we also need an instructor to lead us through life! We know that God provides for us a divine instructor. Listen to what Jesus said, "When He, the Spirit of truth, comes, He will guide you into all the truth" (John 16:13, *NASB*). Truth is found in the person of Jesus our Savior. The agent of truth that separates us from our old ways is the person of the Holy Spirit. The Spirit teaches us how to use all that Jesus provides for us and activates His work in us.

Paul said that the Corinthian believers were a "letter from Christ [that is, authored by Christ] . . . written not with ink but with the Spirit of the living God, not on tablets of stone but on tablets of human hearts" (2 Corinthians 3:3). Jesus displays His life in our lives through the workings of the Holy Spirit. Because the Holy Spirit has access to our hearts, He becomes the "Spirit of life" (Romans 8:2) and the one who "gives life" (2 Corinthians 3:6). The Spirit's ministry is summed up in the prophet Ezekiel's promise of His coming: "I will give you a new heart and put a new spirit in you. . . . I will put my Spirit in you and move you to follow my decrees and be careful to keep my laws" (Ezekiel 36:26-27).

It is our job to center our minds on Christ and to listen to the leading of the Holy Spirit. Christ empowers us and the Spirit guides us. Every part of our Christian walk is performed through the work of the Spirit. Check out these verses:

We love by the Spirit (see Romans 15:30; Colossians 1:8).

We are sanctified by the Spirit (see Romans 15:16; 1 Corinthians 6:11).

We pray by the Spirit (see Romans 8:26; Ephesians 6:18).

We hope by the power of the Spirit (see Romans 15:13).

By the Spirit we put to death the misdeeds of the body (see Romans 8:13).

We are led by the Spirit (see Romans 8:14; Galatians 5:18).

We worship in the Spirit (see Philippians 3:3).

We are strengthened by the Spirit (see Ephesians 3:16).

We walk according to the Spirit (see Romans 8:4; Galatians 5:16).

We are taught by the Spirit (see 1 Corinthians 2:13; 1 John 2:20,27).

We produce good fruit by the Spirit (see Galatians 5:22-23).

We could list many more things that the Holy Spirit does in our lives as believers, but this small list conveys that our growth is not accomplished by our own effort, but rather by the power of the Holy Spirit at work inside us.

It is absolutely essential, therefore, that we be as sensitive as we can to the voice of the Holy Spirit and His gentle leading. The Bible gives us four important commands that we are to obey when it comes to responding to the Holy Spirit. Two of those commands are positive: "Walk by the Spirit" (Galatians 5:16, *NASB*) and "Be filled with the Spirit" (Ephesians 5:18). And two commands are negative: "Do not grieve the Holy Spirit" (Ephesians 4:30) and "Do not quench the Spirit" (1 Thessalonians 5:19, *NASB*). We need to ask ourselves, "Am I obeying those commands?" If we're not, there is no way we can enjoy a right relationship with God and continue to become more like Christ.

Paul tells us to "walk by the Spirit"(Galatians 5:16, *NASB*). Life is pictured as a "way" on which a person journeys. How a person lives his or her life is considered to be the way he or she walks. So "to walk" means simply to live or conduct life.

The Bible calls believers to walk in a certain way of life—so much so that in New Testament times, Christians were known as followers of the Way (see Acts 9:2; 22:4). Before we knew Christ, we did whatever we wanted. We didn't walk like Jesus or exhibit a supernatural lifestyle. In fact, the Bible says that we "walked according to the course of this world, according to the prince of the power of the air" (Ephesians 2:2, *NASB*); "according to the flesh" (Romans 8:4, *NASB*); "like mere men" (1 Corinthians 3:3); "in the darkness" (1 John 1:6; 2:11).

Now we are to walk in Christ (see Colossians 2:6); "in the light" (1 John 1:7); "as children of light" (Ephesians 5:8); "according to love" (Romans 14:15, *NASB*); "in the same manner as [Jesus] walked" (1 John 2:6, *NASB*); and "according to the Spirit" (Romans 8:4).

How is it possible to live this way? It certainly isn't possible in the flesh. It's only possible because of our position in Christ. Through the Holy Spirit living in us, we can learn to hear the voice of God and walk in the Spirit. There is no way we will ever stop living in the flesh or operating in the power of our own wisdom until we surrender control of our lives to the Spirit. Remember, God isn't asking us to walk in the Spirit just on Sundays, but rather every moment of every day. God's Word promises us that when we walk by the Spirit, we won't carry out the desires of the flesh, because the flesh sets its desires against the Spirit and the Spirit is against the flesh (see Galatians 5:16-17).

Are you walking hand in hand with the Spirit today? Or is the flesh winning? Today, you have everything you need to submit to the Spirit and follow His plan. The question is, Will you?

Remember the tragic story of John F. Kennedy, Jr.? He needed a guide that day. If we ignore God's instructions, Christ's example and the Holy Spirit, we'll crash as well. If we listen, we'll reach new heights beyond anything we might imagine.

Discussion

- Every aspect of our Christian life is performed by the what?
- In addition to living by the Spirit, what other things does the Spirit do in our life? Name at least three.
- Scripture gives us four commands about our relationship with the Spirit. What are they?

The Lie to Reject

I reject the lie that I can put down the ways of the flesh by my own wisdom or willpower.

The Truth to Accept

I accept the truth that if I walk by the Spirit, I will not carry out the desires of the flesh.

Prayer

Dear heavenly Father, according to the Bible, a godly man walks as if he were always before You. Lord, I know that You are everywhere and that Your Spirit lives in me, so I am ever before You. You told Abraham, "I am God Almighty; walk before me and be blameless" [Genesis 17:1]. *Lord, I desire to walk before You blameless, so I choose to devote myself totally to You! In Jesus' name I pray. Amen.*

Reading

1 Corinthians 13:1-13

Inhibiting the Work of the Spirit

Do not quench the Spirit.
1 Thessalonians 5:19, *NASB*

The Holy Spirit is not just a little piece of God—He is God. God dwells in us as believers. The Bible even says that we are sealed. In other words, God has stamped His holy character on us (see Ephesians 1:3-14; 4:30). The Bible commands us to walk by the Spirit—to live under the Spirit's total control. We do this by staying in fellowship with the Spirit, following His promptings and fulfilling God's desires. If we choose, through our free will, to ignore the Spirit's wishes, then we are grieving the Spirit or quenching it. The Spirit, like an alarm, will tell us when we are letting sin come between our fellowship with God (see Ephesians 4:30). We also grieve the Holy Spirit when we tear down others rather than build them up. Grieving carries with it the idea of causing physical or emotional pain. In other words, we are causing God pain when we ignore His loving leading. Why do we do that? The answer, quite frankly, is sin. Isaiah 63:9-10 reads, "In his love and mercy he redeemed them; he lifted them up and carried them all the days of old. Yet they rebelled and grieved his Holy Spirit."

When we quench the Spirit, not only do we wound God's heart, but also we build up a barrier between the Spirit and us. As a result, the ministry of the Spirit isn't able to flow through our lives and encourage others around us. God's Word says, "Do not quench the Spirit" (1 Thessalonians 5:19, *NASB*). But what if we already have? The truth is that we all have quenched the Spirit at times. Here is a story that will give us the right perspective and a place to start when we realize that we have quenched the Spirit.

Recently my dad and younger brother Joel attended a party for Stephen Taylor, one of Joel's best friends. It was a very special occasion. Stephen was turning thirteen, and his dad wanted to make Stephen's entrance into young adulthood memorable. Nice presents wouldn't suffice; Stephen's dad wanted to impart wisdom. To accomplish this he asked fathers to accompany their sons to the party and to bring a special gift—a tool that served them in their specific lines of work.

Each father gave his tool to Stephen along with its accompanying "life lesson" for the "toolbox" of principles Stephen would carry into life. The tools were as unique as the men who used them. My dad gave Stephen a quality writing pen and explained that a pen not only served him when he wrote his ideas but also represented his word when he signed an agreement.

During the gift giving, a father who was a professional homebuilder handed Stephen a small box. "Inside that box is the tool I use most," he said. Stephen opened it and found a nail puller.

"My nail puller, simple as it might seem," the father explained, "is one of the most important tools I have." This father told the story of how once, while in the middle of building a wall, he discovered that it was crooked. Instead of halting the construction and undoing a little work to fix the wall, he decided to proceed, hoping that the problem would go away as he continued to build. However, the problem only worsened. Eventually, at a great loss of materials and time, he had to tear down the nearly completed wall and totally rebuild it.

"Stephen," the father said gravely, "times will come in life when you'll realize you've made a mistake. At that moment, you have two choices: You can swallow your pride and 'pull a few nails,' or you can foolishly continue your course, hoping the problem will go away. Most of the time the problem will only get worse. I'm giving you this tool to remind you of this principle: When you realize you've made a mistake, the best thing you can do is tear it down and start over."[23]

God's Spirit will help us know which nails to pull if we listen to the Spirit's leading and don't quench the Spirit. The Spirit's awesome role in our lives is often described as fire: "Do not put out the Spirit's fire" (1 Thessalonians 5:19). The way to put out fire is to throw water on it or withhold its fuel. In the same way we can cut off the Spirit's work in our lives by ignoring His leading.

When we find a nail in our lives that needs to be pulled, we're being sensitive to the presence of sin. Such sensitivity is one of the major ways we can walk in the Spirit. We're called to come out of the darkness and walk in the light so that we can experience forgiveness and restoration. Scripture says, "Everything that does not come from faith is sin" (Romans 14:23). In other words, whatever we do by faith that is not based in truth is sin and hinders the Spirit's ministry in our lives. In the same way, John says, "Everything in the world—the cravings of sinful man, the lust of his eyes and the boasting of what he has and does—comes not from the Father but from the world" (1 John 2:16).

What goes on in our mind and all our actions are either coming from a work of the Spirit, or they are coming from this fallen world. God's Word asks us to renounce all our worldliness, even our human wisdom (see 1 Corinthians 1:20–2:5), our human standards (see 1 Corinthians 2:14-15) and all human righteousness (see Philippians 3:9). Walking by the Spirit is asking God to search our hearts and let us know if there is any "hurtful way in [us]" (Psalm 139:23-24, *NASB*). Whenever we find the nails of sin that are hindering the Spirit's ministry in us, we must deal with them in a biblical way. Here's how we do that:

1. Repent and confess (see 1 John 1:9). We need to openly agree with God that we have sinned and turn from our sinful ways.
2. Recognize and receive God's gracious forgiveness on the basis that Christ's work on the cross satisfied the punishment for our sins. The apostle John said that God is "faithful and just and will forgive us our sins and purify us from all unrighteousness" (1 John 1:9).

There is a peace that the world can't give but comes when we walk in step with the Spirit. When we quench the Spirit, everything is out of sorts.

Today you have a choice to make. Do you want a day that seems all out of sorts or a day that is filled with peace? What do you think is worth more than peace? If you have lived without peace for very long at all, you have probably discovered that no amount of sinful pleasure is worth surrendering the peace that God offers us. God loves you and cares for you so much that He has provided a way for all of your sins to be taken away. Now it is up to you to walk in the freedom that He has provided.

Discussion

- Paul's first negative command about our relationship with the Spirit is that we "not grieve the Holy Spirit of God" (Ephesians 4:30). What does this mean?
- What is true repentance? What is true confession?
- Why are recognizing and receiving God's gracious forgiveness so important?

The Lie to Reject

I reject the lie that I can sin all I want and still not grieve the Spirit.

The Truth to Accept

I accept the truth that because of Jesus, God always loves me and wants me to walk with Him.

Prayer

Dear heavenly Father, I know that at times I grieve Your Holy Spirit. Please forgive me for the times I fail. Lord, I desire to walk in step with Your Spirit. Please reveal to me anything that keeps me from following You and Your ways! In Jesus' name I pray. Amen.

Reading

1 Corinthians 14:1-10

Being Filled
with the Spirit

Be filled with the Spirit.
Ephesians 5:18

Yesterday we learned how to avoid putting up roadblocks to the Holy Spirit's ministry through the command to not quench the Spirit. Today's verse goes further, asking us to be proactive by being filled with the Spirit. "To be filled" means to come under the Holy Spirit's complete control. When we are filled with the Spirit, we won't respond to hurtful things in our lives the way world would. That is a lesson that a 14-year-old girl named Anne Tait learned from her brother. It is a lesson that each of us needs to learn from the Spirit of God.

Sometimes the lessons that you learn in life come from the people you least expect them from. My little brother, Jimmy, is twelve years old. He's also mentally and physically handicapped. He had a stroke before he was born and parts of his body (his toes and his brain) didn't completely form.

But even though those things aren't completely what they should be, I think Jimmy made up for it in the area of his heart. When we go out in public, there are people who stare at us, who won't even come near us, because they're afraid—afraid of my baby brother.

I've seen kids as little as four stick out their tongues and make evil little faces at him as though he weren't even human. But Jimmy never gets angry. He doesn't bear them up or hate them forever. He just gives them a big old grin.

It's amazing to watch. First, his big, brown eyes grow sparkly, and the corners of his mouth begin to twitch. Then, when his smile does break, and his small, white teeth peek through those lips, it's as if the sun has broken through the clouds.

Some people say they feel sorry for Jimmy and that it's too bad he isn't "normal." But you know what? In a way, I wish everyone on this earth was [sic] like my brother. Because no matter how mean people are to him, he always has a smile.

So now, if people are mean to me or make fun of me, I just give them a big old grin, because I've learned from my little brother that it's not how much your brain has developed, or how many toes you have, it's how much your heart feels and how big a smile you wear.[24]

We are filled with the Spirit when we surrender control of our thoughts and actions to God so that He can manifest His presence. Paul said that a Christian's life ought to be characterized by the abiding presence of the Spirit displayed in his or her life (see Acts 6:3).

We are choosing the Spirit's way when we get rid of our own selfish desires and embrace God's plan—when we give up trying to provide for ourselves and trust God to meet our needs. Jesus will always pass by the self-sufficient—those who want to live through their own power. Check out Mark 6:48, *NASB*:

> Seeing them straining at the oars, for the wind was against them,
> . . . He intended to pass by them. But when they saw Him walking on the sea, they supposed that it was a ghost, and cried out;
> for they . . . were terrified. . . . Immediately He spoke . . . "Take courage; it is I, do not be afraid."

For the Holy Spirit to be able to fill your heart, your heart first has to be emptied of self-interest and self-sufficiency. Let us illustrate. Imagine you have a glass filled with water and suddenly you decide to have a glass of milk instead. Obviously, you have to pour out the water first or you'll make a big mess. In the same way, the Holy Spirit can only fill what is empty. Paul said, "The one who sows to his own flesh will from the flesh reap corruption, but the one who sows to the Spirit will from the Spirit reap eternal life" (Galatians 6:8, *NASB*). Today you have a choice. You can surrender to the Spirit and experience the supernatural life of Christ or you can try to fake it. Paul said in Romans 8:5 (*NASB*): "Those who are according to the flesh set their minds on the things of the flesh, but those who are according to the Spirit, the things of the Spirit."

Paul was talking about two kinds of people: those who haven't trusted Christ, whose lives are controlled by the flesh; and those who have been born again and are now related to the Spirit of God. We are called to set our minds in a certain way of thinking—God's way! We're called to think on spiritual things. That's what Paul was talking about when he said we are to set our minds "on the things above, not on things that are on earth" (Colossians 3:2).

If we truly want to be filled with the Spirit, we need to concentrate on three important and essential activities: prayer, understanding God's Word and fellowship with other believers. If we want to be in the Spirit's control, we must be students of the Word, people of prayer and active members of our churches.

Prayer. The Spirit helps us to know how to pray and how to pray more effectively (see Romans 8:26-27). In fact, life in the Spirit is a life of unceasing prayer (see 1 Thessalonians 5:17). Paul tells us, "*Pray* in the Spirit on all occasions with all kinds of *prayers* and requests. With this in mind, be alert and always keep on *praying* for all the saints. *Pray* also for me" (Ephesians 6:18-19, emphasis added). Without prayer, we can't be filled with the Spirit.

Understanding God's Word. Being filled with the Spirit is also the same as being filled with God's Word. The command "be filled with the Spirit" in Ephesians 5:18 is parallel to Paul's command in Colossians 3:16 (*NASB*): "Let the word of Christ richly dwell within you." Walking in the Spirit helps us relate to the rest of the Body of Christ. It is the Spirit that helps us share Christ and witness to the lost (see Acts 1:8). It is the Spirit who provides every believer with a spiritual gift. These spiritual gifts are designed to help the Body grow and become more like Christ (see 1 Corinthians 12).

Attending church. Today, by reading this devotional, you have spent time in the Word and time in prayer. Add interaction with the Body of Christ, and you have the recipe for being filled with the Holy Spirit. Ask the Lord whom He wants you to encourage today. You may encourage that person through a phone call or an e-mail. But nothing is like personal fellowship. Allow God to use you to brighten someone's day, and you'll find that your day will brighten as well.

Discussion

- To be "filled with the Spirit" means to let the Spirit who lives in us, manifest in what ways?

- We make room for the Spirit's filling by emptying ourselves of what?
- For a person to set his or her mind on something means more than thinking a certain way. It also means to make something an absorbing interest that involves what three things?
- Being filled with the Spirit is also the same as being filled with what?

The Lie to Reject

I reject the lie that I can let my mind dwell on sin and still please the Spirit.

The Truth to Accept

I accept the truth that I must set my mind on the ways of the Spirit so that I can walk free.

Prayer

Dear heavenly Father, I want to be filled with Your Spirit. I want to be completely controlled and sealed by the Spirit's power. I know that in the past I have filled my life with so many things that were not important. Some of those things were even wrong and sinful. Please forgive me. I choose to turn from those things and to turn to You. Please fill me with Your Spirit's strength and love today. In Jesus' name I pray. Amen.

Reading

1 Corinthians 14:11-25

The Yearning to Be Filled

*When he, the Spirit of truth, comes, he will
guide you into all truth.*
John 16:13

Walking in the truth is absolutely necessary for us in order to be filled with the Spirit. Sometimes we are tempted to let little lies or little deceptions go. But a *little* lie is like having just a *little* cancer or being bitten by a *little* dog. A lie is still a lie. If we want to be filled by the Spirit, then we have to walk in the truth. Here is a story that shows how easy it is for deceptions to get started.

> I read about the twenty-year reunion of most of those who helped form the old American Football League. The seasoned sports veterans and owners swapped stories and enjoyed a full evening of laughs and reflections together.
>
> Among those present was Al Davis, longtime owner of the Oakland Raiders. He looked at all those sitting at his table and recalled an eventful evening back in 1959 when they all stared with envy at Nicky Hilton, the scheduled speaker. On that long-ago night everyone's feelings of expectation rose another notch when Hilton was introduced as having recently made $100,000 in the baseball business in the city of Los Angeles. Hilton stood to his feet as the place broke into thunderous applause. When he stepped to the microphone, however, he said he needed to correct the details of his introduction. It was not he who'd enjoyed that experience, but his brother Baron. And it wasn't Los Angeles, but rather San Diego. And it wasn't baseball, but football. And it wasn't $100,000, it was $1 million. And he didn't make it, he *lost* it.[25]

They had every fact wrong! They even had the wrong guy. Is your life like Nicky's? If it is, you need to do what he did and walk in the light. Set the record straight. Augustine, a fourth-century church leader, tells us that in his early years his attitude was "Lord, save me from my sins—but not yet." Jesus said, "You will know the truth, and the truth will set you *free*" (John 8:32, emphasis added). The truth is not an enemy seeking to expose us—it is a liberating friend! If we want to be filled with the Spirit, we must have a genuine desire to live a holy life.

Jesus also said, "Men loved darkness instead of light because their deeds were evil" (John 3:19). The Lord loves us too much to allow us to hide, cover up and walk in darkness. We may fear exposure, but that fear is not from God. The Holy Spirit will guide us out of darkness and into the light, where we can enjoy fellowship with God and other believers. He is first and foremost the Spirit of truth, and He will lead us into all truth. Our responsibility is to respond to that truth by faith.

The Bible says, "In the gospel a righteousness from God is revealed, a righteousness that is by faith from first to last, just as it is written: 'The righteous will live by faith'" (Romans 1:17). The process of salvation, from beginning to end, is a matter of living by faith. Growth in sanctification, therefore, may be summed up as growing in the exercise of faith. We live by faith (see Habakkuk 2:4; Galatians 2:20; Hebrews 10:38), and we walk by faith (see 2 Corinthians 5:7, *NASB*). "The only thing that counts is faith expressing itself through love" (Galatians 5:6). We overcome the world by faith (see 1 John 5:4). The flaming arrows of the evil one are extinguished by the shield of faith (see Ephesians 6:16). Living victoriously in Christ is the "good fight of the faith" (1 Timothy 6:12). And we are kept for the final salvation by the power of God through faith (see 1 Peter 1:5).

Faith is the lifeline that connects us to God. Faith is the avenue through which God invades our lives. Faith in God, then, is manifest by actions that are in harmony with our relationship with Him. By faith we pray and seek to hear His voice through the Word and the Spirit. By faith we are obedient to the law of Christ. If we say that we have faith but fail to practice those things, we are deceiving ourselves.

Faith is simply responding to God—responding to what He does or says. When Mary learned that she had been chosen to be the mother of Jesus, her response, "May it be to me as you have said" (Luke 1:38), was a response of faith. She was simply responding to God's revealed Word. When we hear God tell us something and we respond, we are exercising our faith.

Living by faith means acting in faith. Some people say that our response should be passive, since the Christian life is in reality Christ living His life in us through the empowerment of the Spirit. They say we should just wait for God's power to act. But faith is an active concept, and living by faith requires us to live in obedience to God. The life of

Christ is visible in us only through our activities of faith.

One of the greatest illustrations of this truth appears in Mark 3:1-6, which tells of Christ healing the man with the shriveled hand. Jesus commanded the man, "Stretch out your hand" (v. 5). The man could have looked at his hand and responded, "No, I can't move it until I feel strength in it." Instead, we are told that "he stretched it out, and his hand was completely restored" (v. 5). Clearly Jesus supplied the power to move the hand, but the avenue by which Christ's power invaded the man's body was the man's own faith.

Philippians 2:12-13 is another Scripture passage that illustrates the connection between our activity in faith and God's enabling power: "Continue to work out your salvation, . . . for it is God who works in you to will and to act according to his good purpose." Even though it is God who moves us to will and to act, we are called to work out that which He does in us. Paul prays for God to perfect the believers at Corinth, yet he also exhorts them to "aim for perfection" (2 Corinthians 13:11). We are commanded to be blameless (see Philippians 2:15), yet it is God who makes us blameless (see 1 Thessalonians 3:13). It is our responsibility to have faith, hope and love; and yet all of these are gifts of God (see John 13:34; Romans 15:13; Ephesians 3:17; Philippians 1:9; 2 Thessalonians 1:11).

Living by faith means obeying God's commands even when they seem contrary to reason. For example, you may have a sin habit that seems unconquerable, but if you believe that the power of Christ is greater than the power of sin, you will take steps in obedience to holiness. In faith you will say, "What God asks for, He will empower me to accomplish through my obedience." When you exercise faith, you are looking past your human weakness and depending fully on the power of Christ's life in you.

It's by faith that we live and grow in holiness. There are two important principles to remember. First, exercising our faith is not the same as exercising our willpower. Living the Christian life and growing in holiness are not accomplished by resolving to conquer the sinful tendencies of the flesh or by the performance of rigid disciplines. The purpose of the spiritual disciplines—prayer, studying God's Word, fellowship, loving acts of service and so on—is to stimulate us to go to Christ for the strength to become holy. They are of no use—in fact they can be hindrances—if they are done with the thought that we can overcome sin by our own power.

Living by faith means that everything in our lives is accomplished by God's grace. We're not saying that God simply helps us to be holy. The Pharisee in Luke 18:9-14 recognized that it was God who had helped him to not be "like other men" (v. 11). Living by genuine faith, however, is different. We do not act to gain life; rather we act out of the fullness of life that is already ours in Christ. All of our desires toward God and all of our activities are ultimately the result of His grace at work in us. We are called to live by faith in the gospel; God has provided a perfect salvation from beginning to end. We believe this reality and act on the basis of it. Peter stated both God's provision and our responsibility in his second epistle:

> His divine power has given us everything we need for life and godliness through our knowledge of him who called us by his own glory and goodness. Through these he has given us his very great and precious promises, so that through them you may participate in the divine nature and escape the corruption in the world caused by evil desires. *For this reason, make every effort to add to your faith* goodness; and to goodness, knowledge; and to knowledge, self-control (2 Peter 1:3-6, emphasis added).

Growing by faith also comes from knowing and meditating on the reality of God and His work for us, in us and through us. Scripture affirms that faith comes through the Word of God (see Romans 10:17). It's in the Word that we see God's works. Jesus, who is the Word, is "the author and perfecter of our faith" (Hebrews 12:2). Indeed, "without faith it is impossible to please God" (Hebrews 11:6).

Discussion

- If we want to be filled with the Spirit, we must have a genuine desire to live how?

- Faith is the avenue through which God invades our lives. Faith in God is manifested by what?
- Faith is simply responding to whom?
- The Bible says that without faith it is impossible to do what?

The Lie to Reject

I reject the lie that I can live the Christian life without faith, hope and love.

The Truth to Accept

I accept the truth that it is my responsibility to have faith, hope and love, and yet all of these are gifts of God.

Prayer

Dear heavenly Father, You said "If anyone is thirsty, let him come to me and drink" [John 7:37]. Lord, I ask that You would create a great thirst in my heart for You and Your Word. You promised that if I believe in You, streams of living water will flow from within me! Lord, I believe in You! I know that Your Spirit lives in me so that I can experience the flow of "living water" and a great "thirst" for You. I know that Your Spirit wants to do great things in my life, so have Your way, Lord! In Jesus' name I pray. Amen.

Reading

1 Corinthians 14:26-40

Growing in Holiness!

You are . . . fellow citizens with God's people and
members of God's household . . . with Christ Jesus himself
as the chief cornerstone. In him the whole building is joined
together and rises to become a holy temple in the Lord.
And in him you too are being built together to become a
dwelling in which God lives by his Spirit.
Ephesians 2:19-22

We've become people who like our privacy. We love to be left alone. In fact, we are a generation of loners. God never designed us, however, to be isolated and separated from fellow believers. We need others in the Body of Christ, and they need us. A big part of our growing up in the Lord is when we decide how much we are going to be involved in the Church. Some students we know take more time picking out their prom outfits than they do seeking God's guidance as to where they should fellowship.

You are going to become like those you hang around. If you hang around strong believers, you'll be stronger. If your friends aren't really concerned about the Lord, you will likely lose your convictions toward God and His ways as well. Even in the beginning when God created man, He said, "It is not good for the man to be alone" (Genesis 2:18).

Becoming more like Christ is not just a matter of our own individual growth. Our sanctification is related to how we grow up in the Body. When the Bible talks about holiness, it uses words like "we" and "our." In other words, God is growing us up as His children in the context of the Body of Christ. In the Bible, the word "saint" is used 60 times in the plural, but only once in the singular.

Are you trying to grow up on your own? It will never happen. Just as wolves can't successfully hunt alone, so we weren't created to grow up by ourselves. Wolves are pack animals. They need each other; in the same way, you and I need each other to grow up and become more like Christ.

We glorify the lifestyle of the lone wolf. But, quite frankly, lone wolves don't live very long. Hebrews 10:24-25 says: "Let us consider how we may spur one another on toward love and good deeds. Let us not give up meeting together, as some are in the habit of doing, but let us encourage one another." When others encourage us in fellowship with the Body of Christ, we are more likely to grow and display the holiness of God, like the boy in this story.

In the days when an ice cream sundae cost much less, a ten-year-old boy entered a hotel coffee shop and sat at a table. A waitress put a glass of water in front of him.

"How much is an ice cream sundae?"

"Fifty cents," replied the waitress.

The little boy pulled his hand out of his pocket and studied a number of coins in it.

"How much is a dish of plain ice cream?" he inquired.

Some people were now waiting for a table and the waitress was a bit impatient. "Thirty-five cents," she said brusquely.

The little boy again counted the coins. "I'll have the plain ice cream," he said. The waitress brought the ice cream, put the bill on the table and walked away. The boy finished the ice cream, paid the cashier and departed. When the waitress came back, she began wiping down the table and then swallowed hard at what she saw. There, placed neatly beside the empty dish were two nickels and five pennies—her tip.[26]

It's that kind of self-sacrifice and serving of others that God desires in our lives so that others can see Christ in us. We need each other because we are created "in the image of God" (Genesis 1:27). Because we bear God's image, we desire fellowship in the same way that Jesus desired fellowship with the Father. God is Triune: the Father, Son and Holy Spirit—three Persons in one personal being. We know with certainty that God is a social being. We are not self-sufficient like God. But like God we have been created with the need and desire for fellowship. When we ignore our natural inward desire to be with other believers, we rob ourselves of the blessings and strength we need to live in a lost and dying world. In fact, to even find out what God is like, we need the Body—people sharing the truths that God has taught them. If we stay isolated and alone, we'll miss the true nature of God. The Body needs you, and you need the Body!

Discussion

- According to the Bible, God intends for us to grow together as part of a community. What is the first verse in the Bible that validates this truth?
- What is our true nature as human beings?
- According to the Bible, God is Triune: the Father, Son and Holy Spirit—three Persons in one personal being. Although we cannot

fully understand the Trinity, we can know with certainty that God is what kind of being?

· What will we miss if we remain isolated and alone?

The Lie to Reject

I reject the lie that I can live alone and still grow in Christ.

The Truth to Accept

I accept the truth that I need the fellowship that the Church offers.

Prayer

Dear heavenly Father, I know that I can't make it through life alone. I need You and the Body of Christ. Help me, Lord, to open up to others and let people see the real me. Lord, I know that You have called to me to a ministry of encouragement, so I need to let people get close to me. Help me to see others as You see them, in Christ. I ask You to use me to encourage and strengthen someone today. In Jesus' name I pray. Amen.

Reading

1 Corinthians 15:1-11

Fellowship Affirms Our Identity

Bring all things in heaven and on earth together
under one head, even Christ.
Ephesians 1:10

I recently had the opportunity to go to Rindi, a game preserve in Africa. As I gazed over the incredible sunlit plains, I had the opportunity to see lions, elephants, baboons and hippos. But the thing that struck me the most was the incredible number of deer and antelope. As far as my eye could see in every direction, were herds of various kinds. As I looked closer, I could see that all the different species had banded together there on the plain as a means of protection from their predators. It was obvious that there were so many eyes on the lookout, no predator could get very close to the herd.

In the same way, we need to protect each other from the schemes of the world, the flesh and the devil. In America, we like to glorify individuality. But it seems lately there are so many people trying to be different that they all look the same. Sometimes we think we lose our individuality when we become part of a group. It is really the other way around. Our uniqueness shines when we are part of the Body of Christ! If we fail to embrace the Body, we become an easy target for sin. If we choose an independent lifestyle, we are more likely to live independently of God. Sin always brings isolation. Isolation destroys our sense of community. Without community, we won't grow up to become like Christ. We may not like everything about community, but its good qualities clearly outweigh the bad. In a way, the Body of Christ is like growing up in a small town. This next story will show you what I mean.

A little town is where everybody knows what everybody is doing—but they read the weekly newspaper to see who got caught at it.

In a little town everybody knows every neighbor's car by sight and most by sound—and also knows when it comes and where it goes.

In a little town there's no use in anybody lying about his age or his ailments or exaggerating about his ancestors or his offspring.

A little town is where, if you get the wrong number, you can talk for 15 minutes anyway—if you want to.

A little town is where there is hardly anything to do and never enough time to do it.

In any town the ratio of good people to bad people is a hundred to one.

In a big town, the hundred are uncomfortable.

In a little town, the "one" simply is.

A little town is where businessmen struggle for survival against suburban shopping centers . . . where they dig deep to support anybody's worthy cause, though they know "anybody" shops mostly at city stores.

Small-town gossip tends to cut down anybody who's up, help up anybody who's down.

The small-town policeman has a first name.

The small-town schoolteacher has the last word.

The small-town preacher is a full-time farmer.

The small-town firemen take turns.

Why would anybody want to live in one of these tiny "blink and you miss it towns"?

I don't know. Maybe because in the class play there's a part for everyone.

In the town jail there's rarely anyone.

In the town cemetery, you're among friends.[27]

Jesus cared a lot about unity. That is why He prayed in the "high priestly prayer" that we all be one as He and the Father are one (see John 17:20-23). The book of Ephesians addresses this as well—it is God's goal "to bring all things in heaven and on earth together under one head, even Christ" (Ephesians 1:10).

The Bible makes it clear that we belong to each other. "We are members of one another" (Ephesians 4:25, *NASB*); "We, who are many, are one body in Christ, and individually members one of another" (Romans 12:5, *NASB*).

This oneness is expressed over and over again in the book of Ephesians:

- We are all "fellow citizens" (Ephesians 2:19).
- We are "joined together and [rise] to become a holy temple" and "built together to become a dwelling in which God lives by his Spirit" (Ephesians 2:21-22).

- The gospel has made us all "heirs together," "members together" and "sharers together" (Ephesians 3:6).

All these verses describe who we are in Christ right now. Because of these truths, we can live in unity with one another as the Body of Christ and become more like Jesus. Paul says:

> Be completely humble and gentle; be patient, bearing with one another in love. Make every effort to keep the unity of the Spirit through the bond of peace. There is one body and one Spirit— just as you were called to one hope when you were called—one Lord, one faith, one baptism; one God and Father of all, who is over all and through all and in all (Ephesians 4:2-6).

Today, make an effort to find out what is going on in the lives of those around you. Just by showing an interest in the lives of others you can promote the unity and Body life that God says we need to further our own sanctification. When you build others up, you get built up. Today make the choice to open yourself up and let others into your life. You won't regret it.

Discussion

- In Western culture, in which we emphasize individuality, we often think that our individuality is lost when we become part of a group. But the opposite is true. Why?
- When we choose to live independently of God, we not only alienate ourselves from the Creator but also from whom?
- Since the Fall, every attempt to unite humanity on any basis other than Jesus Christ has ended how? Why do you think that is the case?

The Lie to Reject

I reject the lie that I can have true unity with others based on anything other than Jesus Christ.

The Truth to Accept

I accept the truth that I am joined together with others in Christ to become a holy temple.

Prayer

Dear heavenly Father, You ask me to be completely humble, gentle and patient, bearing with others in love. Lord, I confess that I'm not always gentle, humble or patient the way I should be. Please forgive me for my selfishness. I want to make every effort to keep the unity of the Spirit through the bond of peace as Your Word says. I know that there is one Body and one Spirit and that You, Lord, are the head. Help me to follow You every day. In Jesus' name I pray. Amen.

Reading

1 Corinthians 15:12-19

Growing Up

May the God who gives endurance and
encouragement give you a spirit of unity among
yourselves as you follow Christ.
Romans 15:5

The last few days we have talked a lot about unity and how we need each other. We need to remember that one day God will call us home to be with Him in a place called heaven. We won't spend eternity alone; rather, we'll spend it in fellowship with God and all of His people. The biblical picture of life in eternity is not one of individual living. The difficulty of living with people now because of sinful self-centeredness may make us hope that heaven is a beautiful place where each of us gets to live alone in our own mansion. But while heaven will no doubt be beautiful and spacious, our eternal home is pictured as a city, the New Jerusalem, where all of God's people live in the richness of human community (see Revelation 21—22). In heaven there will be a total absence of sin, and the unconditional love and acceptance that we find in our heavenly Father will finally be perfected in us.

We live in a day of individualism that too often inserts itself into the concept of spiritual growth. We usually seek to build up ourselves, and this may cause us to desire little attachment to the community of believers. And sometimes the attachment we do seek is motivated by a desire to enrich ourselves!

The devil wants us to stay isolated. He begins his plans by encouraging us to isolate ourselves from the rest of the Christian community so that we have no accountability, and sin is inevitable once we start to live independently of God and each other.

At a men's retreat, after I (Neil) spoke on the importance of being willing to forgive others, two brothers approached me. Both had been married and then remarried. One of the brothers hadn't been to church for seven years. He said, "Neil, my problem is canonicity [a reference to the process by which early Christian leaders determined which books belonged in the Bible]. I have read seven books on the closing of the canon, and I just can't accept what evangelicals say about this."

I had no idea there were seven books on the subject of canonicity, but I also knew that his real struggle had nothing to do with the closing of the canon. I got off the subject as fast as I could and got to what he was really struggling with, which turned out to be his need to come to terms with his past. He had never known his birth father, and his stepfather had never spent time with him. Thus, he had never had a father. The result was that he had never developed close relationships with anyone. The same was true about his brother.

Those men were not alone; there are many young people who have never learned to relate to others on a personal basis. I soon learned that the brothers had never experienced any sense of intimacy with their spouses or with other Christians, much less God. For them, church was an academic exercise, and marriage was nothing more than two people living in the same house. One brother had already left the Church, and both were in danger of losing their second marriages—all because they had never known any bonding relationships.

When I explained the necessity of relating intimately with God and one another, the one brother who hadn't left the Church decided the conversation was getting too personal. So he left. The other brother knew in his heart that intimacy was what he had lacked in his church experience and his present marriage, as well as his failed marriage.

That night he had an encounter with God in a way he had never known before. The next morning he was still red-eyed from repenting, forgiving and connecting with His heavenly Father. He asked to share his heart with the rest of the men through music. By the time he was done, there wasn't a dry eye in the camp. This dear man, like too many children of God, had kept other Christians and family members at an arm's length. When we do that, we rob ourselves of what God has given the Body of Christ, which can only be received when we relate to one another.

It is easy to see that spiritual growth means growth in our ability to live in peace with others. Almost all the "deeds of the flesh" (Galatians 5:19-21, *NASB*) cause discord, while the fruit of the Spirit (see Galatians 5:22-23) encourage close relationships. Growth in our spiritual life means growth in our personal relationships. This growth in our relationships is not simply the goal of individual growth, as if a person could first grow in isolation and then get along with others better.

Consider this illustration of the importance of fellowship: A wooden tub requires good staves to hold water (a stave is a narrow strip of wood or iron covering or lining a vessel). If the individual staves are shrunken and dried up, the tub can no longer serve its purpose. Similarly, the Church must have healthy members in order to be unified and fulfill its purpose. Keep in mind that it's not enough for the wood staves to each be healthy; they must also work together toward a common goal: keeping the water inside the tub. God's design for us in His plan of salvation is that we become healthy, not only individually through direct personal relationship with Him, but also through vital relationships with others.

Paul said that we "are being built together to become a dwelling in which God lives by his Spirit" (Ephesians 2:22). He was not talking about people who are growing individually but a group of believers who are unified through their relationships. Peter described us as "living stones" all united to "the living Stone" being built into one "spiritual house" (see 1 Peter 2:4-5).

You were designed to build others up, so who are you going to build up today?

Discussion

- What is the biblical picture of what life is like in eternity?
- Who wants us to stay isolated from other believers? Why?
- In the Bible, spiritual growth means growth in our ability to live in harmony with whom?
- List the names of people you will build up today.

The Lie to Reject

I reject the lie that heaven is an isolated, self-serving place.

The Truth to Accept

I accept the truth that heaven is an awesome place where all of God's people live in the richness of human community.

Prayer

Dear heavenly Father, I am so used to living for myself! Please forgive me for my selfishness. Help me to think of the needs of others, to care for them and to put their needs first. Lord, I know that when I serve others I'm acting like Jesus and build-ing up His kingdom. Lord, help me not to live in isolation and loneliness. I need You and the family You have given me in Christ. Sometimes it's so easy to just pull in and stay away from others, but that's not what You want. So I choose today to open myself up and let other people in. Lord, I'm going to stop protecting myself. I ask You to protect me. In Jesus' name I pray. Amen.

Reading

1 Corinthians 15:20-34

Relationships
and Bearing Fruit

*We are to grow up in all aspects into Him, who is the head,
even Christ, from whom the whole body, being fitted and held
together by that which every joint supplies, according to the
proper working of each individual part, causes the growth
of the body for the building up of itself in love.*
Ephesians 4:15-16

Have you ever heard a good joke? A good joke isn't as funny when you are alone, right? The larger the group, the funnier the joke is. In the same way, we need relationships as believers to see the fruit of the Spirit (see Galatians 5:22-23). The knowledge of spiritual matters is not gained alone. Rather, it is gained through interaction with other believers. Paul prayed that we as believers "may have power, together with all the saints, to grasp how wide and long and high and deep is the love of Christ, and to know this love that surpasses knowledge—that you may be filled to the measure of all the fullness of God" (Ephesians 3:18-19).

Clare De Long shares an incredible story about how life brings along circumstances that force us to need each other. Through that dependence we build pathways of friendship and love. It is on these pathways that we also grow up.

> Looking out through our kitchen window we can see a path from our porch through the grass to the property adjoining ours. That property belongs to my mother—that path also belongs to her.
>
> Some time ago, I was involved in a near fatal car accident. With nine bones broken and other injuries, I needed constant care and my future recovery meant a possible stay in a rehabilitation center.
>
> My husband decided a few days before my discharge to take me home. The doctor approved and the equipment that would be needed was shipped and set up in the spare bedroom. Wally and Mom had accepted the responsibility of caring for me twenty-four hours a day.
>
> That's when her path began. It continued to be used every day. For the next two-and-a-half months, Mom traveled that path in sunshine, rain, snow and sleet during the morning and afternoon hours, even sometimes in the middle of the night.
>
> I call it her path of love. The things she did for me at that time are as many as the stars in the sky. She cared for me as only a mother could. Her love, tenderness, and gentleness shown to me will never be forgotten. Eighteen months later the path remains a visible sign of a mother's love.[28]

In Ephesians 4:12-16, Paul once again talks about how maturity in faith and knowledge takes place when those in the Body of Christ are involved in building up one another. As each of us contributes our part to the rest of the Body, we come to a better understanding of the spiritual matters that help to nourish our life and growth.

God conveys Himself to each of us, not only through our personal relations with Him and our practice of the spiritual disciplines, but also through other believers as we fellowship with them. Now that we understand the truth that fellowship contributes to our growth, let's look at how this happens.

The fact that we grow through relationships can be seen clearly in Paul's picture of the growing Body in Ephesians 4. Paul begins his discussion of our growth by saying that "each one of us" has received a grace gift from God (Ephesians 4:7). The nature and purpose of those gifts becomes evident when he describes the purpose of giving us evangelists and pastor-teachers (see Ephesians 4:11). These gifted people are called "to prepare God's people for works of service [ministry], so that the body of Christ may be built up" (Ephesians 4:12). This tells us that the building up of the Body of Christ is the result of the ministry of all believers.

The Bible's analogy of the Body becomes even more interesting when we consider that nearly every cell in our physical body will die and be replaced within seven years, except for the cells in our brain and spinal cord, which constitute our central nervous system. On the spiritual side of the analogy, Christ is the head of the Body and the Holy Spirit completes the central nervous system. They never change, and they ensure the proper provision and direction for the rest of the Body, which is being renewed continuously. The Church Body would cease being a living organism without their presence.

This same truth is portrayed in Paul's discussion of spiritual gifts in 1 Corinthians 12. There he talks about the various members of the Body and how they are all needed, not only for the proper functioning of the entire Body, but also for the proper functioning of each other. "The eye cannot say to the hand, 'I don't need you!' And the head cannot say to the feet, 'I don't need you!'" (1 Corinthians 12:21). Just as the parts of our physical bodies need each other, so also do the members of Christ's Body need each other. We are designed and equipped by God to minister what God has given to each of us for the health and growth of other believers. We cannot grow properly apart from our contact with them.

Paul describes the Body as "being fitted and held together" through the ministry of each member (Ephesians 4:16, *NASB*). In the New Testament era, builders used an elaborate process to fit stones together. They cut and then rubbed the surfaces of the stones together to remove any rough edges that might keep them from fitting together perfectly. Then holes were drilled and dowels prepared so that the stones could be even more solidly joined together.

God doesn't just want us to grow up individually; rather, He wants the whole Body of Christ to grow up and mature. The source of all growth is God Himself communicated through His Son, the head of the Body.

What are your gifts? How are you using them to build up the Body? Are you building any pathways of love? Remember, it is on those pathways that you grow as well.

Discussion

- The necessity of relationships among believers is seen in what (see Galatians 5:22-23)?
- Spiritual growth is more than personal. What is it?
- God conveys Himself to each of us not only through our personal relations with Him and our practice of the spiritual disciplines but also through other believers as we enter into what?
- God's goal for humanity is not simply a number of perfected individuals but a humanity that is perfected and what?

The Lie to Reject

I reject the lie that I can grow on my own apart from the Body of Christ.

The Truth to Accept

I accept the truth that the source of all growth is God Himself communicated through His Son, the head of the Body.

Prayer

Dear heavenly Father, thank You that I am growing up in all aspects into Christ, who is the head. Thank You, Lord, that I am being fitted and held together by the Church, Your Body, which is like muscles and joints working together. Lord, You cause the whole Body to grow up in You, and You are building us up in love and unity. Thank You for building me up and letting me fit in. In Jesus' name I pray. Amen.

Reading

1 Corinthians 15:35-50

Encouraging Growth

[The Early Church] committed themselves to the
teaching of the apostles, the life together, the
common meal, and the prayers.
Acts 2:42, *THE MESSAGE*

One important way we can minister to each other is through prayer. Jesus Himself prayed for others, including Peter in Luke 22:31-32, and all believers in John 17:9-24. Paul also prayed constantly for others (see Ephesians 3:14-19). Although many of the Bible's instructions about prayer may refer to private prayer, the context of many of those passages suggests praying together as well (see Romans 12:10-13; 1 Thessalonians 5:14-17; James 5:13-16; 1 Peter 4:7-10). Praying together helps us to avoid praying selfishly, because it forces us to focus on others and God's work in general.

It is the mark of Spirit-filled believers to "speak to one another with psalms, hymns and spiritual songs" (Ephesians 5:19; see also Colossians 3:16). The effect of such ministry was once demonstrated to me (Neil) in a most remarkable way. A college student had asked me to visit her dying grandmother, who was not a Christian. She had slipped into a coma that she was not expected to come out of, and she was given only a few more days to live because the family had given permission for removal of all the life-support systems.

I could hear the grandmother's labored breathing as I entered her room. My student was supposed to meet me there, but she hadn't arrived yet. The grandmother's eyes were crossed, and every attempt to communicate with her was met with no response. I silently prayed for wisdom because I had no idea what to do. Then the Holy Spirit distinctly impressed upon my mind that I should sing to her. His prompting was clear, and I was glad there was no one else in the room. Feeling a little self-conscious, I knelt by the elderly woman's bed and began to sing Christian songs. Suddenly her eyes came together, and I could sense that she was consciously hearing me. During the next few minutes I had the privilege of leading this dear woman to Christ. Then her granddaughter came into the room, returning from the cafeteria, where she had been with her mother. I shared with them what had just happened. We praised God as we looked at the student's grandmother, who was smiling at us with tears rolling down her cheeks. She lived for two more years. The family asked me to speak at the funeral service, which resulted in many more people coming to Christ.

We are told to do good to all, but especially to those in the family of believers (see Galatians 6:10). We are also told to practice hospitality, which is a love of strangers (see 1 Peter 4:9).

Giving is another way that we can minister to one another for the growth of all. Reread today's opening passage. These practices all took place in the context of a church body. The dynamics at work in the fellowship among believers are much the same as those with any group of people, except that the interaction is not merely human. Rather, the supernatural life of Christ is being shared through the power of the Spirit. It is because of Christ's life that we receive spiritual nourishment.

You have probably heard before that the more strands you have in a cord, the stronger it is. Alone, you are just a single thread and could easily snap or break when a small pressure or trial comes. Thousands of threads wound together can bear an incredible burden. We become strong when we fellowship with others. If we stand alone, then Satan's lies and the world's trickery will easily stretch us too far. When we are with like-minded people who understand God's Word and seek God's voice, we will become stronger than we imagine.

Roman soldiers in the New Testament times used a huge, door-shaped body shield that could provide much individual protection. But even more protection was offered when the soldiers came together as a compact unit and held these large shields side-by-side in front of them or above them. If they stood apart and held their shields individually, their sides were exposed, but when they brought their shields together, they were more fully protected. How strong is *our* faith together? The Bible paints a neat picture for us using what is called the shield of faith (see Ephesians 6:16).

When we fellowship together, we set up the perfect environment for our own spiritual growth. Discipleship cannot take place unless a disciple has a mentor. Have you opened your life up to those in the Body who are a little further down the road than you are? Seek out mature individuals whose lives are filled with the love of Christ, and learn from them. Remember, nobody has it all together. The point is to simply get to the place where iron can sharpen iron. Because none of us can boast about having every spiritual gift, there is a sense in which we naturally need each other so that we can partake of all that God has for us. We also need to learn from other people's experiences and perspectives. Don't just observe people—get involved in their lives so that you can see the truths of God actually modeled. That is far more powerful than simply knowing a fact or truth about God. As it says in the letter to the Hebrews, we should "encourage one another daily" (Hebrews 3:13).

Whom can you encourage and pray for today? You might even want to pray with someone who needs encouragement.

Discussion

- Although many scriptural instructions about prayer probably refer to private prayer, the context of many of those passages suggests what kind of prayer (see Romans 12:10-13)?
- Corporate prayer helps us to avoid praying selfishly because it makes us focus on what?
- What role do psalms, hymns and spiritual songs play in the life of a believer?
- Why is sharing mutual beliefs and values with one another in close fellowship so important?

The Lie to Reject

I reject the lie that I can perceive all God's truth on my own.

The Truth to Accept

I accept the truth that we need each other in the Body because no one person has all the spiritual gifts.

Prayer

Dear heavenly Father, we are told to do good to all, but especially to those in the family of believers [see Galatians 6:10]. Lord, I confess that many times I don't think of others at church or in the youth group who have needs. I usually think of myself. Help me to get my eyes off myself and onto You and others. Lord, in 1 Peter 4:9 You said that we are also to practice hospitality, which is the love of strangers.

Help me today to show Christ to a lost and dying world. In Jesus' name I pray. Amen.

Reading

1 Corinthians 15:51-58

The Keys to Great Fellowship

As God's chosen people, holy and dearly loved,
clothe yourselves with compassion, kindness, humility, gentleness
and patience. Bear with each other and forgive whatever
grievances you may have against one another. Forgive as the
Lord forgave you. And over all these virtues put on love, which
binds them all together in perfect unity.
Colossians 3:12-14

Ever wonder why geese fly in a V formation? Scientists at the California Institute of Technology did—they put their computers and flight simulators to work and discovered the answer—flocks of geese form this pattern because it's the easiest way to fly.

The formation acts aerodynamically like a single wing; that is, wind drag is distributed equally across all the birds. This in turn reduces drag on each individual bird. Twenty-five geese flying together in a V can travel seventy percent farther than one goose flying alone.

Because the lead goose actually situates itself slightly behind the perfect point position of the V, the geese that follow relieve some of its wing drag. It does not have to work harder than the others.

The benefit of the airflow pattern in the V (because it acts as a single flying wing) goes both ways. While the lead birds pull along those that are behind, the followers' flight sends relief back up to the front.

From geese we can learn that, although we live in a society that promotes individualism and self-reliance, we function more effectively in community. Like the geese, we were created by God to work together, serve together, and encourage and support each other. When we cooperate and help each other to succeed, we not only accomplish much, but we do it with less stress and difficulty. Let's do it God's way.[29]

It is through relationships that God primarily does His great work of transforming us into the image of Christ. Paul lays out in the book of Colossians the importance of community. First, Paul tells us about Christ and His finished work. Jesus left nothing undone when He left Earth to return to heaven. Paul then talks about establishing and building believers up in Christ. Paul wraps it up by finally telling us about what a mature believer acts like. Let's take a minute to review what Colossians is talking about.

In chapters 1 and 2 we learn that we are placed into the kingdom of Christ, forgiven and established in Him. Awesome news isn't it! But there is even more good news. Those same chapters tell us that Satan has been defeated by Christ's work on the cross. Chapter 3 begins with the challenge to set our eyes on the things of above, and to put off the old man and put on the new man, "which is being renewed in knowledge in the image of its Creator. Here there is no Greek or Jew, circumcised or uncircumcised, barbarian, Scythian, slave or free, but Christ is all, and is in all" (Colossians 3:10-11). In other words, there should be no racial, religious, social or cultural barriers in the Body of Christ. We are unified in Him.

After establishing who we are in Christ, Paul gives us some hints for developing character. Look what Paul says about character one more time (see Colossians 3:12-14) Notice what these verses emphasize.

1. Conform to the Image of God

We can't point our finger at others and blame them for our poor behavior, or say "the devil made me do it." No one can hinder us from becoming the people God created us to be. We have to take responsibility for our characters and actions: No one can control the thoughts we let inside our heads except us. Paul made it clear: "It is God's will that you should be sanctified" (1 Thessalonians 4:3).

2. Love One Another

How do we love others? We do this by accepting one another as Christ accepted us (see Roman 15:7), and laying down our lives for one another as Christ laid down His life for us (see 1 John 3:16). That sounds radical! It is radical, and the world will notice if we show that kind of powerful love. That's the whole point! Imagine what would happen in your youth group if everyone assumed responsibility for his or her own growth in character, and made a commitment to meet one another's needs.

Discussion

- There should be no racial, religious, social or cultural barriers in the Body of Christ. Why?

- Why are there barriers in the Body of Christ today? What can be done to eliminate those barriers?
- Why can't we blame other people for hindering us from becoming the people God created us to be?
- What would happen in our homes and our churches if everybody assumed responsibility for his or her own growth in character, and everybody made a commitment to meet one another's needs?

The Lie to Reject

I reject the lie that others have to meet my needs and that others are responsible for my growth.

The Truth to Accept

I accept the truth that I am responsible for my own growth in character. I am also committed to helping meet the needs of others.

Prayer

Dear heavenly Father, I do wonder what would happen in my home, school and church if everybody assumed responsibility for his or her own growth in character, and everybody made a commitment to meet one another's needs. It would be so awesome. Lord, help me to do my part and grow up in You. I want to help others grow up in You, so I ask You to use me today to help meet someone else's needs. Jesus' name I pray. Amen.

Reading

1 Corinthians 16:1-9

The Struggle!

*Brethren, we are under obligation, not to the flesh,
to live according to the flesh—for if you are living according to
the flesh, you must die; but if by the Spirit you are putting to
death the deeds of the body, you will live. For all who are being
led by the Spirit of God, these are sons of God.*
Romans 8:12-14, *NASB*

It's true that our ability to become like Christ is a miracle and that can sometimes lead us to believe that we don't play a role in the process of sanctification. Some think that we should let go and let God do all the work. But we have a responsibility to submit to God's control, to rest in His power and to keep our eyes on Him. Joni Eareckson Tada shares a personal experience that I think will show you how important our role is.

When I was little and went horseback riding with my sisters, I had a hard time keeping up. My problem was that I was riding a little pony only half the size of their mounts. I had to gallop twice as fast just to keep up.

I didn't mind. I took it as a challenge—until we came to the edge of a river. My sisters on their big horses thought it was fun and exciting to cross the river at the deepest part. They never seemed to notice that my little pony sank quite a bit deeper into the swirling waters. It was scary, but I wasn't about to let them know.

One crossing in particular sticks in my memory: the Gorsuch Switch Crossing on the Patapsco River. It had rained earlier that week and the river was brown and swollen. As our horses waded out toward midstream, I became transfixed staring at the swirling waters rushing around the legs of my pony. It made me scared and dizzy. I began to lose my balance in the saddle.

The voice of my sister Jay finally broke through my panic. "Look up, Joni! Keep looking up!"

Sure enough, as soon as I focused on my sister on the other side, I was able to regain my balance and finish the crossing.

That little story came to mind recently when I was reading about Peter in Matthew 14. It seems he had a similar problem as he walked on the water toward the Lord Jesus. He looked down at the raging waters, got dizzy, and lost his balance. Because he took his eyes off the Lord and put them on the swirling waves around him, he began to sink.

How much we are like him! Instead of resting on the Word of God, we let our circumstances almost transfix us, absorbing us to the point where we begin to lose our spiritual equilibrium. We become dizzy with fear and anxiety. And before you know it, we've lost balance.

It's easy to panic, isn't it? And admittedly, it's hard to look up—especially when you feel like you're sinking.

But my pony and I made it across the Patapsco and Peter made it back to his boat. Thousands before you, enduring the gale force winds of circumstance, have made it through, keeping their eyes on the Lord Jesus. How about you?

If you can't find a way out, try looking up.[30]

It's true that our victory over sin is only possible because of the work that Christ accomplished on the cross. Our progressive sanctification won't occur, however, if we don't keep our eyes and focus on Jesus. We must abide in Him and submit to the power of the Holy Spirit. When Peter tried to walk on the water on his own, he sank. But when he declared his dependence on Christ and submitted to the power of God, he found victory. The same is true for us. God is the one who brings about our spiritual growth (see 1 Corinthians 3:6). We can rest on the finished work of Jesus, but we also need to do our part. God has done His part by providing for us complete forgiveness and unconditional acceptance. We can rest in the fact that we don't need to perform good deeds to earn God's love. But it is God's desire that we do far more than just lie around basking in His love. He wants us to show the world the work that Christ has done in our lives. Paul's tells us to "work out your salvation with fear and trembling" even as God "works in you to will and to act according to his good purpose" (Philippians 2:12-13). God prepared our "good works . . . in advance for us to do," but we are still to do them (Ephesians 2:10).

Maybe you have heard the old cliché, "Every Christian is like a diamond in the rough." In other words, we used to be just a lump of coal. How does a lump of coal become a diamond anyway? I am no geologist, but the process requires the right balance of time and pressure, along with the absence of impurities. If there are any foreign elements or impurities present, no amount of time or pressure will turn the coal into a diamond. Christ, through His death on the cross, removed all our impurities. We have been justified. Now God is sanctifying us through time and the pressures we face.

It is over time and through the pressures of life that we work out our salvation with the fear and trembling that Paul was talking about. Paul said the Christian life is like a race, and that we should run so as to win: "Forgetting what is behind and straining toward what is ahead, I press on toward the goal to win the prize for which God has called me heavenward in Christ Jesus" (Philippians 3:13-14). Paul also tackles this metaphor here:

> Do you not know that in a race all the runners run, but only one gets the prize? Run in such a way as to get the prize. Everyone who competes in the games goes into strict training. They do it to get a crown that will not last; but we do it to get a crown that will last forever. Therefore I do not run like a man running aimlessly; I do not fight like a man beating the air. No, I beat my body and make it my slave so that after I have preached to others, I myself will not be disqualified for the prize (1 Corinthians 9:24-27).

Every professional football player has to attend training camp. Even the greatest quarterbacks, like John Elway, Dan Marino, Joe Montana and Brett Favre, have to attend and go through the rigorous practice drills. Even though they are the best in the league and have won bowl games, their coach expects them to drill again and again until each play is executed to perfection. What if Elway said, "I'm a pro. I have dozens of passing records. I don't need to practice"? First, his attitude would be a real detriment to his team. Other players would say, "If he's not practicing, then I'm not going to practice." Second, no coach would put up with that kind of insubordination. The reason those men will go down as some of the greatest quarterbacks to have ever played the game is because they were willing to take their natural talents and hone them through continual training. If men are willing to have that kind of commitment to something as insignificant as a game of football, how should we view our commitment to the game of life? We need to daily practice living like Christ until we can execute His plans perfectly. We'll score more than touchdowns, and the records that are put down in God's heavenly score book will bring eternal rewards.

Paul also said, "Train yourself to be godly" (1 Timothy 4:7). We get the English word "gymnasium" from the Greek word for "train," which, in 1 Timothy 4:7, suggests rigorous exercise in things related to godliness. Sanctification requires us to ground ourselves in the basics of our faith and then discipline ourselves to live according to what God says is true.

Whether we like it or not, we are in a battle against evil forces (see Ephesians 6:10-16)—a battle that is described as a "struggle" in verse 12, or literally, a "wrestling." The Greek word describes a "hand-to-hand fight." Paul wrote to Timothy, "I give you this instruction in keeping with the prophecies once made about you, so that by following them you may fight the good fight" (1 Timothy 1:18). Later he added, "You, man of God, flee from all this, and pursue righteousness, godliness, faith, love, endurance and gentleness. Fight the good fight of the faith" (1 Timothy 6:11-12). In his second letter to Timothy, he said, "Endure hardship with us like a good soldier" (2 Timothy 2:3). Then at the end of his ministry, Paul said, "I have fought the good fight, I have finished the race" (2 Timothy 4:7). Those instructions reveal that the Christian life is not at all an effortless lifestyle. Keep your eyes on Jesus and fight to win!

Discussion

- Victory over sin is possible only through the finished work of Christ. Why do you think it is important to "train" ourselves in the basics of our faith?
- Paul tells us to work out our "salvation with fear and trembling." What does he mean?
- Sanctification requires us to ground ourselves in the basics of what?
- What are the things we as humans struggle with? What do you struggle with?

The Lie to Reject

I reject the lie that the Christian life is always easy and battle free.

The Truth to Accept

I accept the truth that I am in a struggle but that Christ has already won the war over sin and death.

Prayer

Dear heavenly Father, I know that I am in a battle between good and evil. My enemies are the world, the flesh and the devil. I am so thankful that You defeated them at the cross. Lord, sometimes I want to give in. Help me to stay strong and not give in to these temptations. Lord, I want to follow You, and I know that with You I can win any battle. So today I choose to submit to You and resist the devil, and I know that when I do, he must flee! In Jesus' name I pray. Amen.

Reading

1 Corinthians 16:10-24

The Traitor Within

*When we walk by the Spirit will we not
carry out the desire of the flesh.*
Galatians 5:16, *NASB*

One of the major roadblocks that we face on the road to maturity is one that is very close to us. As a matter of fact, it is within us. The Bible says that our "flesh" has sinful desires that work against God's plan. When we accepted Christ, we received a new nature; but our flesh is still present and, if left unopposed, it can interrupt God's work of sanctification. Paul wrote, "With my flesh [I am serving] the law of sin" (Romans 7:25; see also v. 18, *NASB*).

When the Bible uses the word "flesh," it can mean the physical body or our desire to sin. A person who walks by the flesh is self-centered rather than God-centered. In short, the flesh seeks life on human terms and standards rather than on God's. It is the human tendency to rely on self rather than God. The Bible doesn't mess around when it talks about how we are to respond to the flesh. It says, "Put no confidence in the flesh" (Philippians 3:3).

When we accepted Christ and God's Spirit set up residency in our hearts, He radically changed how we relate to the flesh. The power of the flesh wasn't eliminated, but we were given what we need to overcome its sinful desires. Before we knew Christ, we didn't have much of a struggle with our flesh because without God's Spirit, there was no conflict. We just did whatever the flesh told us to do, and we didn't have a problem with it. With God's presence involved, however, our inner person, or who we are in Christ, now recognizes that some of the flesh's activities are not in alignment with God's character. In other words, our flesh wants us to do things that Jesus wouldn't do. The Holy Spirit rings the bell and the fight is on. The Bible says, "Those who live according to the sinful nature have their minds set on what that nature desires. . . . The sinful mind is hostile to God. It does not submit to God's law, nor can it do so. Those controlled by the sinful nature cannot please God" (Romans 8:5,7-8).

Because we have accepted Christ and we are "in Him," sin's power through the flesh has been destroyed. We "are not in the flesh but in the Spirit" (Romans 8:9, *NASB*). In our death with Christ we made a radical break with the flesh. Paul said, "Those who belong to Christ Jesus have crucified the flesh with its passions and desires" (Galatians 5:24, *NASB*).

There is no way we can live out the life of Christ while allowing our flesh to control and reign in our lives. Even our good intentions and best efforts will be fouled up. It is kind of like the little girl in this story who had the right idea, but she still saw one fouled-up detail ruin the whole surprise.

> There was a mother who was sick in bed with the flu. Her darling daughter wanted so much to be a good nurse. She fluffed the pillows and brought a magazine for her mother to read. And then she even showed up with a surprise cup of tea.
>
> "Why, you're such a sweetheart," the mother said as she drank the tea. "I didn't know you even knew how to make tea."
>
> "Oh yes," the little girl replied. "I learned by watching you. I put the tea leaves in the pan and then I put in the water, and I boiled it, and then I strained it into a cup. But I couldn't find a strainer, so I used the flyswatter instead."
>
> "You what?" the mother screamed.
>
> And the little girl said, "Oh, don't worry, Mom, I didn't use the new flyswatter. I used the old one."[31]

Just like the young girl, we often have good intentions; but if we listen to the flesh, things will come out like tea strained through a used flyswatter. As Christians, we no longer have to listen to the flesh or its call. The flesh no longer has dominant control in our lives. God is the One running the show. By submitting to His Spirit and ignoring the flesh and its sinful input, we can walk and display our new identity in Christ. The flesh, with its sinful passions and desires, is present to tempt us to indulge in self-centered attitudes and actions. That's why we are told to "walk by the Spirit, and [we] will not carry out the desire of the flesh" (Galatians 5:16, *NASB*).

The flesh acts like our friend, but in reality it's a traitor within us whose self-centered desires are the display of sin's tempting power. Paul said that before he became a follower of Jesus, he tried to gain life according to the flesh:

> If anyone else has a mind to put confidence in the flesh, I far more: circumcised the eighth day, of the nation of Israel, of the

tribe of Benjamin, a Hebrew of Hebrews; as to the Law, a Pharisee; as to zeal, a persecutor of the church; as to the righteousness which is in the Law, found blameless (Philippians 3:4-6, *NASB*).

After Paul became a Christian, instead of putting his confidence in the flesh, he gloried in Christ (see Philippians 3:3) and boasted in the Cross (see Galatians 6:14). The flesh is the constant desire to avoid living life through the Cross or to gain true life through giving up our self-centeredness.

The Bible clearly shows that we are vulnerable to the sinful desires of the traitor within—the flesh. That's why the Bible is filled with commands to avoid the attitudes and actions of the flesh both in our personal and church life. But we do not have to give in to the flesh, because we are no longer dominated by its desires. Today the flesh will do some talking. Will you listen to the flesh or the Spirit?

Discussion

- We will experience more intense struggles with our flesh as the enemy of God now that we are Christians. Why?
- Paul said, "Those who belong to Christ Jesus have crucified the flesh with its passions and desires" (Galatians 5:24). If the flesh has been crucified, why do we still have trouble with it?
- After Paul became a Christian, instead of putting his "confidence in the flesh," he gloried in Christ (Philippians 3:3) and boasted in what (see Galatians 6:14)?

The Lie to Reject

I reject the lie that I have to listen to the flesh and its call.

The Truth to Accept

I accept the truth that sin's reign over me through the passions and desires of the flesh has been broken.

Prayer

Dear heavenly Father, thank You that we as believers no longer have to live "in the flesh" or have to listen to its call. Sin's reign over us through the passions and desires of the flesh has been broken. Lord, I confess that I often let the flesh have its way. Please forgive me for not focusing on You and who I am in Christ. I choose today to crucify the flesh and follow the leading of the Holy Spirit. In Jesus' name I pray. Amen.

Reading

Colossians 1:1-14

Resisting the Flesh

Those who live according to the sinful nature [flesh] have their minds set on what that nature desires; but those who live in accordance with the Spirit have their minds set on what the Spirit desires. The mind of sinful man is death, but the mind controlled by the spirit is life and peace.
Romans 8:5-6

If we are ever to win the battle with the flesh, we first need to understand that the power to overcome the self-centered life is not found in our own strength. It comes from a power beyond us. Even though we have trusted Christ, we can't overcome the power of sin through the flesh any more than someone who doesn't know Christ can. Without drawing on God's strength, we are just as powerless against sin as those who don't know Him. We must depend on the power that comes from the Holy Spirit. When we do, victory is ours. The Bible says that we can overcome the flesh through the power of the Spirit (see Romans 8:13). Only when we walk by the Spirit will we not "carry out the desire of the flesh" (Galatians 5:16, *NASB*).

Oftentimes when we are walking in the flesh, we actually think we are performing great spiritual feats. Frequently those around us can recognize that it is just the flesh at work. But we may think that we have it all together and are doing exactly what God wants, when in reality we can never fulfill God's plans and desires by submitting to the flesh. It is like the young boy in this story. He thought he was doing a great job, but his actions didn't match his understanding of the situation.

> Johnny was very excited. It was the first time he had ever been asked to do something this important. As the wedding music began to play he imagined just how he should carry the pillow with two shiny rings tied on top. Just before touching him on the shoulder to give him the cue to walk down the aisle, his mother looked down and smiled into the upturned face of her four-year-old son. "Don't worry, Mommy," Johnny implored, "I'll do a good job."
>
> Then Johnny took a deep breath, furrowed his brow, bared his teeth and said Grrrrrrr! Everyone turned to face the back of the church. Where was that strange noise coming from?
>
> Johnny growled all the louder and much to Mrs. Smith's surprise, who was sitting on the third pew from the back, he ran up to her and struck her feathered hat with the pillow. His mother looked on in horror. Johnny was fast. He ran back and forth from pew to pew growling and making menacing faces.

Upon reaching the front of the church, Johnny composed himself and gently held up the pillow so the pastor, nonplussed at the performance, could remove the rings. The rest of the ceremony went off without a hitch.

During the reception, the pastor walked up to Johnny who was getting his second piece of wedding cake. "Say, Johnny, what were you doing while bringing the rings to me?"

"My job," declared Johnny proudly, "They asked me to be the Ring Bear!"[32]

It is only through the Spirit that we can discern whether we are truly fulfilling the Spirit's plan. Only by not carrying out the desires of the flesh can we walk in the Spirit. The Bible says:

> If you have been raised up with Christ, keep seeking the things above, where Christ is, seated at the right hand of God. Set your mind on the things above, not on the things that are on earth. For you have died and your life is hidden with Christ in God (Colossians 3:1-3, *NASB*).

If we focus on earthly things, we will likely carry out the desires of the flesh. One girl who attended one of our seminars described well the struggles we can encounter:

> I struggled for my whole Christian life with bizarre thoughts. These thoughts were too embarrassing to share with anyone. How could I admit to someone in the church what had just crossed my mind? I didn't know yet what it meant to take every thought captive to the obedience of Christ. I tried to do it one time, but I was unsuccessful because I still blamed myself for my struggles. I always had a terrible cloud hanging over my head because of this, and consequently I never thought I was righteous because I never felt righteous.
>
> As a result of abuse, I was taught not to think for myself. This set me up for Satan's mind games. I used to fear taking control of

my mind because I didn't know what would happen. I believed that I would lose my identity because I wouldn't have anyone to tell me how to live. But now that I have taken control of my mind, I have gained my identity for the first time. I no longer believe my mother's lies about me, nor the garbage that Satan feeds me. Now I know that I am a child of God. I used to worry about whether a thought came from me or from Satan. Now I realize that is not the issue. I just need to examine the thought according to the Word of God, and then choose the truth.

Only when we understand and internalize the truth and the character of Jesus do we see the ugliness of the flesh. A heart set apart for God will always choose freedom instead of bondage. Only then can we seek out and put an end to the displays of the self-centered life.

Think of it this way: Have you ever seen a big slobbery dog with a bone? How do you get an old bone away from a big hungry dog? You don't want to reach in with your hand and try to take it away—you'll pull back a bloody stump! Also, the dog will become even more protective of his bone. What if you were dangling a 20-ounce T-bone steak with fat dripping off as you pulled it piping hot from the grill? I guarantee you, he'd spit out that old bone so fast it would make your head spin. But because he is a dog, he'll bury that old bone just in case times get lean in the future.

As believers, God wants us to bury the works of the flesh and to take a good look at Jesus when we are tempted to dig them up. Nothing else will satisfy like Jesus: "Blessed are those who hunger and thirst for righteousness, for they shall be satisfied" (Matthew 5:6, *NASB*).

Paul tells us in Romans 13:14 (*NASB*), "Put on the Lord Jesus Christ, and make no provision for the flesh in regard to its lusts." We are not to think of or do anything that might build up the flesh's sinful desires. Letting our thoughts dwell on negative things or immoral subjects can stir up attitudes of anger, envy, bitterness and despair, and lead to immoral actions. If we try to avoid thinking wrong thoughts, however, we will usually end up defeated. Instead, we have to think right thoughts. We are to overcome the lie by choosing the truth. Just renouncing the lie itself will not help us.

Paul told young Timothy, "Flee the evil desires of youth, and pursue righteousness, faith, love and peace, along with those who call on the Lord out of a pure heart. Don't have anything to do with foolish and stupid arguments, because you know they produce quarrels" (2 Timothy 2:22-23).

We are to pursue the things of the Spirit in the fellowship of others. Fellowship with others is important because we're more vulnerable to sin when we are alone. One way of not making provision for the flesh is to stay in ongoing fellowship with other believers.

When I (Neil) was in the Navy, I saw more than one sailor return to the ship beat up and stripped of his money. This happened to sailors who had ventured out alone to a bar during shore leave. I never saw that happen to anyone who had gone with a group of friends to the Christian servicemen's center or to the gym on the Navy base. Likewise, as Christians, we have a choice of either avoiding compromising situations or putting ourselves in them. "Do not be misled: Bad company corrupts good character" (1 Corinthians 15:33).

Discussion

- The power to resist the self-centered life comes from what?
- In the Bible, the believer is told to take two specific actions against the flesh. What are they?
- Why do you think that people with addictive behaviors have no peace of mind?
- If we try to avoid thinking wrong thoughts, we will usually end up defeated. Instead, what should we do?
- Why is fellowship with others so important when it comes to defeating the flesh?

The Lie to Reject

I reject the lie that I can live a life of victory over the flesh without any help from others.

The Truth to Accept

I accept the truth that I need ongoing fellowship with other believers so that I won't make any provisions for the flesh.

Prayer

Dear heavenly Father, You told us to set our minds on the things above, not on the things that are on Earth. For You have died and my life is hidden with Christ in God. Lord, thank You for placing me in Christ and for freeing me from the power of sin. Help me to set my mind on You and Your truth so that I won't carry out the desires of the flesh. In Jesus' name I pray. Amen.

Reading

Colossians 1:15-29

Opposition from Outside

This is the victory that has overcome the world,
even our faith. Who is it that overcomes the world? Only he
who believes that Jesus is the Son of God.

1 John 5:4-5

Not only do we have to fight with the flesh, which is the traitor within, but we also need to stand against the world. The evil character of the world is against God. But this shouldn't surprise us. Jesus said, "If the world hates you, keep in mind that it hated me first" (John 15:18). The wisdom of the world looks at the cross of Christ as foolishness (see 1 Corinthians 1:18-24). The evil nature of the world is seen also in the fact that it is the domain of Satan's rule. He is "the prince of this world" (John 12:31; 16:11) and the "god of this world" (2 Corinthians 4:4, *NASB*). "The whole world is under the control of the evil one" (1 John 5:19). Not only the devil but also his evil spirit allies are spoken of as the rulers, the authorities and the powers of this dark world (see Ephesians 6:12).

What the world is really like is seen in 1 John 2:16 (*NASB*): "All that is in the world, the lust of the flesh and the lust of the eyes and the boastful pride of life, is not from the Father, but is from the world." The "lust of the flesh" is the sinful desires of our fallen human nature—those that leave out God and His will. The "lust of the eyes" relates to looking only on the outward appearance of someone or something without seeing the real value of the person or thing. In the Bible, we read that Eve saw the forbidden fruit as "pleasing to the eye" (Genesis 3:6). Achan saw the forbidden spoils of war and hid them in his tent (see Joshua 7:21). David looked on the beauty of Bathsheba and sinned big-time (see 2 Samuel 11:2-15)!

When John wrote about the lust of the flesh, the lust of the eyes and the pride of the world, he said that those characteristics come "not from the Father but from the world" (1 John 2:16). He was making it clear that the danger of worldliness in our lives is not simply a matter of doing certain things and avoiding others. Rather, he was talking about the attitude we have in life. Is God included in all that we do? If not, then what we do is probably from the world.

The world is also characterized by its own wisdom, which originates from both arrogant human thinking—or pride (see 1 Corinthians 1:19-31)—and the devil (see James 3:15). The world's wisdom talks a lot about knowledge but does not really change lives. James wrote, "Who is wise and understanding among you? Let him show it by his good life, by deeds done in the humility that comes from [true] wisdom" (James 3:13).

The big danger for us as Christians is that we might let our affections be drawn to the world. We are warned, "Do not love the world or anything in the world. If anyone loves the world, the love of the Father is not in him" (1 John 2:15). Demas is an example of someone who failed in his walk as a believer because "he loved this world" and he deserted Paul (2 Timothy 4:10). The world constantly seeks to pull our love away from Christ by appealing to our flesh, which desires to live after the world's values. The connection between our flesh and the world is evident in Paul's description of those who "followed the ways of this world . . . gratifying the cravings of our sinful nature and following its desires and thoughts" (Ephesians 2:2-3). James tells us that both fighting and quarreling—which characterize the world and result from selfishness—come from "your desires that battle within you" (James 4:1).

The world system promotes self-sufficiency and broadcasts this message everywhere in our society and culture—on TV, on the radio and at school. Despite being surrounded by the world's system and having the flesh within us, which is attracted to the world's ways, we have all the resources we need "in Christ" to withstand these threats.

As Christians, having a love for God is possible because in Christ we overcome the world: "This is love for God: to obey his commands. And his commands are not burdensome, for everyone born of God overcomes the world" (1 John 5:3-4). John then shares that the means of victory is our faith in God: "This is the victory that has overcome the world, even our faith. Who is it that overcomes the world? Only he who believes that Jesus is the Son of God" (1 John 5:4-5). Christ's total triumph over the powers of sin belongs to every believer. When we placed our faith in Christ, we, in a very real sense, became overcomers. We have overcome the evil spirit of the world "because the one who is in [us] is greater than the one who is in the world" (1 John 4:4).

Paul said, "Do not conform any longer to the pattern of this world, but be transformed by the renewing of your mind" (Romans 12:2). The focus of renewing our minds has to be on Christ, the author and perfecter of our faith, because He is the way and the truth. Elsewhere, Paul cautions, "See to it that no one takes you captive through hollow and deceptive philosophy, which depends on human tradition and the basic principles of this world rather than on Christ" (Colossians 2:8). We can protect ourselves from the world with the help of all biblical truth, but there are several specific truths that are particularly useful for combating the world.

James said, "Don't you know that friendship with the world is hatred toward God? Anyone who chooses to be a friend of the world becomes an enemy of God" (James 4:4). We cannot serve two masters or love two wives; we must continually recognize how much the world hates God and how much God hates the sin of the world.

Faith in Christ means faith in the Cross. The world hates the Cross because it reveals the ultimate error of the world's attitude that people are adequate and capable of finding life on their own terms. But believers love the Cross. Our confidence is in the Cross alone, and thus, the Cross is our boast. Through the Cross we became radically new creatures that no longer belong to the world or live according to it. We have a new identity, which has absolutely nothing to do with the world. As a result of our crucifixion with Christ, our new identity is not only separate from the world, but it also has new desires, new passions and new values. The faith in the One who overcame the world never forgets the Cross and the new identity that is made possible through His work—an identity completely opposite of the values and characteristics of the world system.

In simple terms, resistance to the world is simply right-mindedness, and worldliness is just plain ignorant! To love the world is to deliberately plan for doom. "The world and its desires pass away [present tense, "are in the process of passing away"], but the man who does the will of God lives forever" (1 John 2:17).

Today we need to realize that we don't need what the world has to offer. We need Christ. Remember this as your day unfolds.

Discussion

- The true characteristics of the world are seen in what key verse?
- We were born into this world physically alive but spiritually dead. We had neither the presence of God in our lives nor the knowledge of His ways. So how were our minds programmed?

- The big danger for Christians is that we might let our affections be drawn to the world. Thus we are warned not to love the world or anything in the world. If we love the world, we won't have a real love for whom? Why not?
- If we have faith in the One who overcame the world, what two things will we never forget?

The Lie to Reject

I reject the lie that I can love the world and its ways and truly love God.

The Truth to Accept

I accept the truth that I cannot serve two masters. I choose to love God and hate sin.

Prayer

Dear heavenly Father, You said that I cannot serve two masters, so I choose to love You and turn from the world and its evil traps. Lord, show me how to recognize the world's traps so that others will see that I really love You. The world hates You, Lord, and everything that You stand for. So I know that it won't be easy to follow You. Still, I choose today to step over the line and be counted as one who is on Your side! In Jesus' name I pray. Amen.

Reading

Colossians 2:1-17

Warfare!

But I am afraid that as the serpent deceived Eve by his craftiness, your minds will be led astray from the simplicity and purity of devotion to Christ.
2 Corinthians 11:3, *NASB*

When we talk about warfare, we are talking about our battle with temptation. Where does temptation come from? Is the devil always the cause of the temptations that we face in our lives? Do temptations come from the sinful world around us? Do temptations come from our own sinful flesh? Frankly, temptations come from all three of them. It's almost impossible to separate these sources of temptation. The devil is not just a figment of our imagination or the Bible's way of identifying our own hunger for sin. The Bible describes Satan as a real being. He is described as the "god of this age" and "the prince of this world." All the world is under his spell.

Paul talked about how the whole world system was being controlled by Satan, and he went on to show how that relates to our flesh. Paul described us before we were saved in this way: "We too all formerly lived in the lusts of our flesh, indulging the desires of the flesh" (Ephesians 2:3, *NASB*). Paul meant that the world and our flesh determined how we lived. Since we were apart from God, we bought right into the world's fallen values and the flesh's evil desires.

All three enemies are at work trying to lure us away from God. It's important that we understand, however, that it is our responsibility to say no to sin. We can't say, "The devil made me do it" or "I couldn't help myself." God is faithful and always provides a way of escape for us (see 1 Corinthians 10:13).

The good news for us is that we are no longer part of the kingdom of darkness. The devil's right to control us was taken away when we accepted Christ. The Bible says that we've been delivered and released from Satan's power (see Acts 26:18; Colossians 1:13). Our champion, Jesus, defeated Satan and all his stinkin' little demons (see John 12:31; 16:11; Colossians 2:15). Now we're connected to Christ in the heavenly realm where Jesus is enthroned. Jesus is "far above all rule and authority, power and dominion" (Ephesians 1:21). Now, because we are in Christ, we have all the equipment we need to fight the spiritual war with the devil and his forces and win (see Ephesians 6:11-18). Nothing, including demons, can separate us from the love of God that is in Christ Jesus our Lord (see Romans 8:38-39). Read how Eugene Peterson said it in his account of Romans from *THE MESSAGE*:

So, what do you think? With God on our side like this, how can we lose? If God didn't hesitate to put everything on the line for us, embracing our condition and exposing himself to the worst by sending his own Son, is there anything else he wouldn't gladly and freely do for us? And who would dare tangle with God by messing with one of God's chosen? Who would dare even to point a finger? The One who died for us—who raised to life for us!—is in the presence of God at this very moment sticking up for us. Do you think anyone is going to be able to drive a wedge between us and Christ's love for us? There is no way! Not trouble, not hard times, not hatred, not hunger, not homelessness, not bullying threats, not backstabbing, not even the worst sins listed in Scripture:

"They kill us in cold blood because they hate you. We're sitting ducks; they pick us off one by one."

None of this fazes us because Jesus loves us. I'm absolutely convinced that nothing—nothing living or dead, angelic or demonic, today or tomorrow, high or low, thinkable or unthinkable—absolutely nothing can get between us and God's love because of the way that Jesus our Master has embraced us.

While all of this is true, the Bible makes it clear that we still have free will and can sin and become enslaved to sin. Our freedom in Christ is real, but we are told to live it out every day.

People are like gloves: A glove can do all sorts of things—pick up a book, wave good-bye, scratch a head, pat someone on the back or slap somebody in the face. This same glove will do nothing if we take our hands out of it, however. All it does is lie there. We can yell at it, get mad at it and try to teach it lessons, but to no avail. It can do nothing on its own. Without our hands inside, the glove is nothing more than an ordinary piece of cloth.

We have choices as to what kind of hand we will put in the glove. If it is worldly, devilish or fleshly, we know how the glove will act. If the glove is filled with the hand of God, then we can expect it to accomplish the same things that Jesus' hands did. People, like gloves, can do little of real consequence on their own. In the flesh we are weak, but with Christ we are strong. When our hands are inside a glove, the glove can do anything our hands want to do. In Philippians 4:13, Paul teaches that we are like gloves: On our own we can do nothing, but with Christ in us, we can do whatever Christ wants us to do. He is the One who gives us the strength and the ability to say no to the world, the flesh and the devil, and yes to God.[33]

The Bible shows us several ways that believers can come under the influence of Satan and his demons. In 2 Corinthians 2:10-11, we are told to forgive because we are aware of Satan's schemes. Paul's hope for those who oppose the Lord's servants is that God would "grant them repentance leading them to a knowledge of the truth, and that they will come to their senses and escape from the trap of the devil, who has taken them captive to do his will" (2 Timothy 2:25-26).

That believers can be influenced is seen in these words from Paul: "In your anger do not sin: Do not let the sun go down while you are still angry, and do not give the devil a foothold" (Ephesians 4:26-27). The word "foothold" literally means "a place." Clearly the matter of a believer's sin is not simply a matter of the flesh; it is also that of the devil as well. While it's clear that we have our enemies, no one can touch our position in Christ, so we have everything we need to walk free today!

Discussion

- What is the cause of our temptations? Is it the world, the flesh or Satan?
- Even though three enemies are involved in attempting to pull us away from God, it is important to note that the final responsibility for our sin rests with whom?
- We as Christians are no longer in the kingdom of darkness, and Satan's power has been broken, but we can still enslave ourselves if we do what?

- How can we make our freedom in Christ real?

The Lie to Reject

I reject the lie that freedom is not real and that I won't be free until I die!

The Truth to Accept

I accept the truth that I have already been proclaimed free.

Prayer

Dear heavenly Father, even though I face three enemies that want to pull me away from You, I know that the final responsibility to say no and close the door on temptation is mine. I know that I can't get away with saying "The devil made me do it." Lord, I look to Your strength and guidance today to see me through. There are so many things that tempt me and want to bring me down. Help me to run from sin and run to You. I pray in Jesus' name. Amen.

Reading

Colossians 2:18-23

Taking a Stand

Submit yourselves, then, to God. Resist the devil,
and he will flee from you.
James 4:7

It is true that we have the devil as an enemy. He is real, and he is power-ful. The big thing to remember is our relationship with God through Christ. Because Jesus outmaneuvered Satan at the cross, we can have confidence that He will outmaneuver him again in every area of our lives. God's Word promises that we can find victory against temptation and the enemy. "Submit yourselves, then, to God. Resist the devil, and he will flee from you" (James 4:7). "Be self-controlled and alert. Your enemy the devil prowls around like a roaring lion looking for someone to devour. Resist him, standing firm in the faith" (1 Peter 5:8-9). The Greek word for "resist" in both verses is literally "stand against."

We are to take our stand in Christ against the devil and his demons. We can't be passive. Instead, we are to be proactive. The Bible tells us to put on the full armor of God:

> Therefore *put on* the full armor of God, so that when the day of evil comes, you may be able to stand your ground, and after you have done everything, to stand. Stand firm then, with the belt of truth buckled around your waist, with the breastplate of righteousness in place, and with your feet fitted with the readiness that comes from the gospel of peace (Ephesians 6:13-15, emphasis added).

We don't battle in the flesh. It is essential that we stay persistent in our pursuit of the Spirit. No matter how often we fail, we need to return to Christ, responding to God's voice and Word with repentance and the willingness to renew our minds. We cannot overstate the importance of going back and rehearsing the truths about who we are in Christ, because it is impossible for us to behave in a way that is inconsistent with how we perceive ourselves. The following story illustrates the importance of our self-perception and of proper understanding of who we are in Christ.

> Jaime Escalante, the Garfield High School teacher on whom the movie *Stand and Deliver* was based, once told me this story about a fellow teacher. During his first year in the classroom, he had two students named Johnny. One was a happy child, an excellent student, a fine citizen. The other Johnny spent much of his time

goofing off and making a nuisance of himself.

When the PTA held its first meeting of the year, a mother came up to this teacher and said, "How's my son, Johnny, getting along?" He assumed she was the mom to better student and replied, "I can't tell you how much I enjoy him. I'm so glad he's in my class."

The next day the problem child came to the teacher and said, "My mom told me what you said about me last night. I haven't ever had a teacher who wanted me in his class."

That day he completed his assignments and brought in his completed homework the next morning. A few weeks later, the "problem" Johnny had become one of this teacher's hardest working students—and one of his best friends. This misbehaving child's life was turned around all because he was mistakenly identified as a good student.

Not every lazy or underachieving boy or girl could be motivated by a simple compliment from a teacher, of course, but there is a principle here that applies to all kids: It's better to make a child stretch to reach your high opinion than stoop to match your disrespect.[34]

If you look closely at the armor of God, you will find that each piece relates very closely to who we are in Christ. We must put on the truths that declare our identity in Him. Putting on the armor of light (see Romans 13:12) is the same as putting on the Lord Jesus Christ (see Romans 13:14). The only safe place we have is "in Christ."

We need to choose truth. Choosing the truth is our first line of defense; therefore, "we take captive every thought to make it obedient to Christ" (2 Corinthians 10:5). We're not supposed to try to analyze whether a thought came from the television set, another person, our own memories or from the demonic. We are to take "every thought" captive. Does that mean we should rebuke every negative thought? No, because we'll find ourselves doing that for the rest of our lives. Instead, we are to overcome the father of lies by choosing the truth. We are not called to dispel the darkness; we are called to turn on the light.

Commitment to God means making ourselves low before Him. Both James 4:6 and 1 Peter 5:5 say, "God opposes the proud but gives grace to the humble." Humility is confidence properly placed. Like Paul, we should "put no confidence in the flesh" (Philippians 3:3). Rather, we should place all our confidence in God. Pride makes us vulnerable to the devil; it is his own sin.

The command that we are to *resist* the devil means that we should not be out looking for trouble, trying to engage the enemy in hostile action. We should never let the devil set the agenda. The Holy Spirit, not the devil, is our guide. Yet at the same time, we should "be self-controlled and alert" (1 Peter 5:8). We are to be aware of Satan's schemes (see 2 Corinthians 2:11).

Spiritual warfare against a spiritual foe requires spiritual weapons. Paul said, "The weapons we fight with are not the weapons of the world. On the contrary, they have divine power to demolish strongholds" (2 Corinthians 10:4). Elsewhere we are told to "put on the full armor of God" (Ephesians 6:11). The Lord Himself used only spiritual weapons (the Word of God) against the devil. We can stand against the power of Satan only by the power of the One who has overcome him—Christ. Abiding in Christ and walking by the Spirit are required for victory in spiritual warfare against the demonic enemy. Spiritual warfare rests on immediate communion with God for fresh power. Paul finished up his words about standing against the enemy with God's armor by saying, "Pray in the Spirit on all occasions with all kinds of prayers and requests. With this in mind, be alert and always keep on praying for all the saints" (Ephesians 6:18).

We should be comforted in the knowledge that Satan's attacks have limitations. He can do only what God permits (see Job 1:11-12; 2:3-6; Luke 22:31), and the battle is the Lord's (see 1 Samuel 17:47). It is part of an ongoing war between good and evil—and the unconquerable One who has already won the war leads us. Christ Himself said, "Take heart! I have overcome the world" (John 16:33). We should be praising God like Paul did: "Thanks be to God! He gives us the victory through our Lord Jesus Christ" (1 Corinthians 15:57).

Discussion

- When we're faced with satanic attacks, the critical issue is our relationship with God. Why?
- First Peter 5:9 says we are to resist the devil: "Resist him, standing firm in the faith." What does that mean?
- Why is there is no place for passivity in the Christian walk when it comes to spiritual conflicts?
- What is our first line of defense?
- Why shouldn't we analyze the origin of every thought that pops into our minds? What should we do instead?

The Lie to Reject

I reject the lie that I don't need God's help or protection against the evil of this world.

The Truth to Accept

I accept the truth that I am in a battle, but I have God's armor to protect me and the battle has already been won in Christ!

Prayer

Dear heavenly Father, You have told us to put on the full armor of God so that when the day of evil comes, I'll be able to stand my ground with the belt of truth, the breastplate of righteousness and the readiness that comes from the gospel of peace. Lord, I choose to put on Your armor today and to clothe myself in Christ Jesus. In Jesus' name I pray. Amen.

Reading

Colossians 3:1-17

When the Going Gets Tough!

Truly, truly, I say to you, unless a grain of wheat
falls into the earth and dies, it remains alone;
but if it dies, it bears much fruit.
John 12:24, *NASB*

In Romans, Paul talks about the trials and tribulations of life and what they produce in our lives: "We also exult in our tribulations, knowing that tribulation brings about perseverance; and perseverance, proven character; and proven character, hope; and hope does not disappoint, because the love of God has been poured out within our hearts through the Holy Spirit who was given to us" (Romans 5:3-5, *NASB*).

The tough times and suffering we run into as we grow from sin toward holiness are inescapable. Yet we can take comfort in knowing that one of the great themes of the Bible is the glory and reward we receive through suffering. Even as we see that Jesus' life was filled with suffering, we shouldn't miss the incredible glory and the profound work that His suffering accomplished. The apostle Paul knew that if he wanted to experience the power of Christ's resurrection as the dynamic force that would transform his life, then he had to endure "the fellowship of sharing in [Christ's] sufferings, becoming like him in his death" (Philippians 3:10).

Some might think, *Can't God perfect us and make us more like Christ in some other way besides suffering?* But the necessity of suffering is made clear in the Bible. We will share in the glory of Christ only if we "share in his sufferings" (Romans 8:17). "If we endure, we will also reign with him" (2 Timothy 2:12; see also 2 Timothy 2:9-10). "For just as the sufferings of Christ flow over into our lives, so also through Christ our comfort overflows" (2 Corinthians 1:5).

Much of the suffering faced by believers is a result of living for Christ in a hostile world. Trials are destined to come "in spreading the gospel of Christ" (1 Thessalonians 3:2). The various trials that bring suffering as a Christian should not be surprising or thought of as strange (see 1 Peter 4:12). Acts 14:22 tells us, "We must go through many hardships to enter the kingdom of God."

None of us is too crazy about the idea of suffering, but the Bible tells us that we can expect it because it is necessary for our spiritual growth. You never know what great things will come about because of our suffering. Check out this true story about a boy who suffered a lot when he was young. When he was older, he was able to use what he had learned in his times of suffering to create something truly incredible!

For Sparky, school was all but impossible. He failed every subject in the eighth grade. He flunked physics in high school, getting a grade of zero.

Sparky also flunked Latin, algebra, and English. He didn't do much better in sports. Although he did manage to make the school's golf team, he promptly lost the only important match of the season. There was a consolation match; he lost that, too.

Throughout his youth, Sparky was awkward socially. He was not actually disliked by the other students; no one cared that much. He was astonished if a classmate ever said hello to him outside of school hours.

There's no way to tell how he might have done at dating. Sparky never once asked a girl to go out in high school. He was too afraid of being turned down.

Sparky was a loser. He, his classmates . . . everyone knew it. So he rolled with it. Sparky had made up his mind early in life that if things were meant to work out, they would. Otherwise he would content himself with what appeared to be his inevitable mediocrity.

However, one thing was important to Sparky—drawing. He was proud of his artwork. Of course, no one else appreciated it. In his senior year of high school, he submitted some cartoons to the editors of the yearbook. The cartoons were turned down. Despite this particular rejection, Sparky was so convinced of his ability that he decided to become a professional artist.

After completing high school, he wrote a letter to Walt Disney Studios. He was told to send some samples of his artwork, and the subject for a cartoon was suggested. He spent a great deal of time on it and on all the other drawings he submitted. Finally, the reply came from Disney Studios. He had been rejected once again. Another loss for the loser.

So, Sparky decided to write his own autobiography in cartoons. He described his childhood self—a little boy loser and chronic underachiever. The cartoon character would soon become famous worldwide.

For Sparky, the boy who had such a lack of success in school and whose work was rejected again and again, was Charles Schulz. He created the "Peanuts" comic strip and the little cartoon character whose kite would never fly and who never succeeded in kicking a football—Charlie Brown.[35]

He suffered a lot in his life, but he became one of the best-loved cartoonists in the world. God uses suffering to produce good things in our lives. Not only are our lives enriched, but so are the lives of those around us. The whole world is a better place because we can open up the Sunday paper and check out what good old Charlie Brown is up to.

It takes suffering in our lives to build character. Jesus is perhaps the best example of this. He was made perfect through suffering (see Hebrews 2:9-10), and "he learned obedience from what he suffered" (Hebrews 5:8). These statements do not suggest that Christ was in some way disobedient or sinful. Rather, the growth He knew through suffering was a growth from immaturity to maturity. He is a compassionate High Priest who can identify with and come to the aid of suffering people (Hebrews 4:15-16). In other words, He can totally relate to us!

You can count on suffering. It may come from the put-downs and anger of the fallen world around us, like the things that Sparky endured. If we are Christ's disciples, we can expect to be persecuted: "If they persecuted me, they will persecute you also," Jesus said (John 15:20). Thus Peter tells the suffering Church of his day, "Do not be surprised at the painful trial you are suffering, as though something strange were happening to you" (1 Peter 4:12).

Today you may suffer. If you do, remember that if you respond to it in the right way, it may begin an incredible work in your life. You might create the next cartoon strip that will replace Charlie Brown. If not, remember this: Those around you are reading your life. Is what they see a work of Christ?

Discussion

• Why does God allow us to go through trials and tribulations?

- What happens if we fail to grow through our trials?
- Give an example from today's devotional that shows how the Lord is patient with us even when we aren't responsive to Him.
- If we are Christ's disciples, we can expect to be persecuted: How have you experienced this persecution? How did that persecution make you feel?
- Looking at your own suffering, what about your experiences has caused your faith in God to grow? How long will this serve you in the future?
- How can you encourage someone today who might be going through a trial?

The Lie to Reject

I reject the lie that I will never experience trials or suffering.

The Truth to Accept

I accept the truth that I will experience trials, but that suffering will make me more like Christ.

Prayer

Dear heavenly Father, You said I should exult in my tribulations, knowing that tribulations bring about perseverance; and perseverance brings proven character; and proven character brings hope. And hope does not disappoint because Your love is poured out in my heart through the Holy Spirit. Help me to respond to You the way I should, even when trials come. Help others see Christ in me today. In Jesus' name I pray. Amen.

Reading

Colossians 3:18-25

God's Great Reward!

We also exult in our tribulations, knowing that tribulation
brings about perseverance; and perseverance, proven character;
and proven character, hope; and hope does not disappoint,
because the love of God has been poured out within our hearts
through the Holy Spirit who was given to us.
Romans 5:3-5, *NASB*

The Bible makes it clear that there is no way for us to go through life without some measure of suffering. In fact, the Bible reminds us that because we have trusted in Christ and bear His name, we will be persecuted (see 2 Timothy 3:12). Our godly life will be offensive to some people around us. And for that we will suffer. We need to look at suffering and understand its work so that we can be directed to become more like Christ. We need to remember that God loves us. He is not punishing us through suffering (see Romans 8:1). Rather, God is acting in love and using suffering to smooth out our rough edges.

We want to remember three things when it comes to suffering.

1. God Is Always in Control of Our Suffering

No matter where suffering comes from, whether it is from God's loving discipline or the hands of a worldly person, we need to remember that it is all under God's control. He is omniscient; He knows everything. God never has to guess what might be good for us. The other thing we need to remember about God is that He is, by His very nature, love. Everything He does, even His discipline, flows out of His infinite love. Therefore, He allows suffering in our lives because it moves us to that place where we can be more like Him. Also, He allows hardships in our lives to bring Him glory. None of us is wise enough to be able to say that we can fully understand the ways of God. We don't know all that He is up to when we are experiencing suffering. It is important, however, that we know that God uses our suffering for our good and to promote His great kingdom work. With this attitude, suffering can produce the greatest growth in our lives and glorify God to the fullest extreme.

2. God Always Limits the Amount of Suffering He Allows

As a father, I (Dave) want my children to grow up and mature. As they get older, I try to give them a little more responsibility as they show me they can handle it. Now that my kids are teenagers, I can entrust them with so many new challenges. But I never would have tested them and challenged them at this level when they were toddlers. In the same way, our heavenly Father sets limits on the suffering that we have to face. God even restricted the amount of suffering that the devil brought into Job's life. Obviously, some saints are able to endure more suffering than others. God knows the limitations that each of us has. We will never be pushed to the point where our suffering would cause us to reject our God and His ways.

> No temptation [testing, trial] has seized you except what is common to man. And God is faithful; he will not let you be tempted beyond what you can bear [beyond your strength]. But when you are tempted, he will also provide a way out so that you can [have strength to] stand up under it (1 Corinthians 10:13).

This promise assures us that God places a limit on our suffering. He knows how much we can bear in each circumstance. He knows the strengths and weaknesses in every area of our lives—physical, emotional and spiritual—and He assures us that He will not allow any suffering on any occasion that we cannot handle with His grace. As parents, like God, we don't want our children to experience fear, insecurity or pain. Yet, it is only through suffering that we will become like Christ.

In times of suffering, do you focus on the storm around you, or do you focus on God? If you focus on the storm, your suffering will bring fear and failure. But if you focus on Christ during the storm, your suffering will produce character and Christlikeness. Tony Campolo shares this light-hearted story about where our focus should be.

> A friend of mine has an adorable four-year-old daughter. She is bright, and she is talkative. If tryouts were being held for a modern-day Shirley Temple, I think she would win, hands down.
>
> One night there was a violent thunderstorm. The lightning flashed and the thunder rumbled—it was one of those terrifying storms that forces everyone to stop and tremble a bit. My friend ran upstairs to his daughter's bedroom to see if she were frightened and to assure her that everything would be all right. He got to her room and found her standing on the windowsill, spread-eagle

against the glass. When he shouted, "What are you doing?" she turned away from the flashing lightning and happily retorted, "I think God is trying to take my picture."[36]

Like the little girl, God will never take us where His grace cannot blanket us and protect us.

3. God Will Always Provide a Way Out

Nowhere in the Bible are we promised that God will keep us from suffering or remove it quickly when it comes. Rather, He promises to provide grace that will enable us to faithfully endure in it. The psalmist did not say, "Cast your cares on the Lord and go free from care," but rather, "Cast your cares on the Lord and he will sustain you" (Psalm 55:22). In the same way, Paul does not tell us that the causes of our worries will be removed, but that in their midst we can be surrounded by God's peace (see Philippians 4:6-7). When Paul was in prison and on trial, he testified, "The Lord stood at my side and gave me strength" (2 Timothy 4:17).

James gives us one of the Bible's most profound statements about suffering, which is often difficult to obey: "Consider it pure joy, my brothers, whenever you face trials of many kinds" (James 1:2). Now, the idea of joy as a result of trials and suffering is not unique to this verse. In Romans 5:3, Paul wrote, "We also rejoice in our sufferings." Similarly, Peter wrote, "Rejoice that you participate in the sufferings of Christ, so that you may be overjoyed when his glory is revealed" (1 Peter 4:13). All of those verses share something of Jesus' blessings of the poor, the mourning, the hungry and the persecuted (see Matthew 5:3-4,6,10-12).

It's important to recognize that we are to express joy in trials—not because of the suffering itself, but because of the outcomes usually associated with suffering. For example, the various sufferings endured by the listeners of Jesus' Beatitudes show that they are rightly related to God and can know the joy that comes from being a part of God's eternal kingdom. This makes them blessed even in the midst of their suffering. In 1 Peter 4:13, Peter spoke of our having joy in our present sufferings with the knowledge that even greater joy is in store for us in the future.

Joy in trials is possible because we are to know that "the testing of [our] faith develops perseverance" (James 1:3). Knowing this, we are to let "perseverance . . . finish its work so that [we] may be mature and complete, not lacking anything" (James 1:4; see also Romans 5:3). Peter tells us that trials produce a genuine faith, like gold from a refiner's fire, which will result "in praise, glory and honor when Jesus Christ is revealed" (1 Peter 1:6-7).

For us to know joy in our suffering, we must have an appreciation—and even gratitude—for what God is doing. We can sense a deep joy in the midst of our trials, not only because we know that they are helping produce godly characteristics within us, but also because we know that God's power is at work in us. Notice what Paul said about God's power in relation to the thorn in his flesh:

> I will boast all the more gladly about my weaknesses, so that Christ's power may rest on me. That is why, for Christ's sake, I delight in weaknesses, in insults, in hardships, in persecutions, in difficulties. For when I am weak, then I am strong (2 Corinthians 12:9-10).

Paul was not rejoicing over his sufferings in the sense that he was seeking more. Rather, he was rejoicing because he knew that through his sufferings, God's power was on display. Sufferings reveal our weaknesses and, thus, are opportunities for God to display His sustaining strength and comfort.

It goes without saying that we cannot find joy in the midst of trials unless we have hope. Paul, Peter and James all indicated that joy could be present in our trials because we have the promise of future glory. The right attitude in suffering is to focus on the hope that is before us.

Some people think that hope is wishful thinking. In actuality, it is the present assurance of some future good. Even though we live in a valley of tears, we can have hope because we know this is not the end. There is a new day coming for the Christian—a day that is described as fullness of joy, where there will be "no more death or mourning or crying or pain, for the old order of things [with its trials and sufferings] has passed away" (Revelation 21:4).

In Romans 5, Paul presented this twofold connection of hope in relation to our suffering. Because of salvation in Christ he declared, "We rejoice in the hope of the glory of God" (Romans 5:2). As believers we are armed with hope as we enter trials and suffering. But then Paul went on to say, "Not only so, but we also rejoice in our sufferings, because we know that suffering produces perseverance; perseverance, character; and character, hope" (Romans 5:3-4). We can more easily accept the sufferings that come our way if we understand that they serve a purpose and if we know that God will make everything right in the end.

Today you might be faced with suffering. Remember, God has allowed it to produce something awesome in your life. Choose today to take your eyes off the storm and put them on Christ and His purpose.

Discussion

· No matter what the source of our suffering—whether directly from God's discipline, from the hand of another person or simply from the evil that is part of the fallen world—it is all under whose control?
· Why is it important for us to realize that God always places limits on our suffering?
· True or false? Nowhere in the Bible are we promised that God will keep us from suffering or remove it quickly when it comes.
· True or false? God promises to provide grace that will enable us to faithfully endure a trial every time we face it.
· Why is it important that we express joy in the midst of suffering?

The Lie to Reject

I reject the lie that God will keep me from ever suffering or remove all my trials quickly when they come.

The Truth to Accept

I accept the truth that God promises to meet my needs and provide all the grace I need to endure every trial I face!

Prayer

Dear heavenly Father, I praise You for Your unfailing love, Your perfect plan and the hope and comfort I find in You. I praise You, too, for the fact that You use and redeem the suffering of my life, and for the ways You've taken care of me in the past. When trials, pain and suffering come again, may I cast my cares upon You and once again know Your grace [see Psalm 55:22]. And, Lord, help me never to doubt in darkness what I have learned in the light about You and Your goodness. Help me also to cling to the hope I have in You so that I will remain faithful and one day see that Your will is indeed good, acceptable and perfect [see Romans 12:2]. Most of all, Lord, help me to willingly accept Your trials so that I may indeed become holy like You. In Jesus' name I pray. Amen.

Reading

Colossians 4:1-18

ENDNOTES

1. "The Lost Treasure," source unknown.
2. Dann Spader and Gary Mayes, *Growing a Healthy Church* (Chicago: Moody Press, 1991), p. 13.
3. Laverne W. Hall, "Faith," in Jack Canfield et al., *Chicken Soup for the Christian Soul* (Deerfield Beach, FL: Health Communications, 1997), pp. 198-199.
4. Alice Gray, comp., "Belonging," *Stories for a Teen's Heart* (Sisters, OR: Multnomah Publishers, 1999), p. 316.
5. *Strong's Exhaustive Concordance of the Bible*, s.v. "dwell."
6. Wayne Rice, "Just a Hyphen," *More Hot Illustrations for Youth Talks* (Grand Rapids, MI: Zondervan Publishing House, 1995), p. 99.
7. Gray, "The Winning Check," *Stories for a Teen's Heart*, p. 240.
8. Gray, "The Saint of Auschwitz," *Stories for a Teen's Heart*, p. 307.
9. Catharine Swift, "Olympic Gold," in Alice Gray, comp., *More Stories for the Heart* (Sisters, OR: Multnomah Publishers, 1997), pp. 94-97.
10. Gray, "Choices," *Stories for a Teen's Heart*, p. 288.
11. Jim Burns and Greg McKinnon, "How to Make a Difference," *Illustrations, Stories and Quotes to Hang Your Message On* (Ventura, CA: Gospel Light, 1997).
12. Bob Benson, "Duty's Dignity," in Alice Gray, comp., *Stories for the Family's Heart* (Sisters, OR: Multnomah Publishers, 1998).
13. Gray, "The Riddle," *Stories for a Teen's Heart*, p. 283.
14. Gray, "The Blind Bomber," *Stories for a Teen's Heart*, p. 79.
15. A. van Selms, *New Bible Dictionary*, J. D. Douglas, ed. (Grand Rapids, MI: Eerdmans, 1962), s.v. "law."
16. See W. E. Vine, *An Expositional Dictionary of New Testament Words* (Old Tappan, NJ: Fleming H. Revell Co., 1966), s.v. "instructor."
17. Gray, "Yerr-Out," *Stories for a Teen's Heart*, p. 242.
18. Chuck Swindoll, "Are You God?" in Gray, *More Stories for a Teen's Heart*, p. 40.
19. Gray, "Not All Valentines Come in Envelopes," *Stories for a Teen's Heart*, p. 21.
20. Gray, "The Blue Ribbon," *Stories for a Teen's Heart*, p. 285.
21. Gray, "Watch Me, Dad," *Stories for a Teen's Heart*, p. 65.
22. Neil T. Anderson and Robert Saucy, *The Common Made Holy* (Eugene, OR: Harvest House Publishers, 1997), pp. 271-272.
23. Gray, "The Toolbox," *Stories for a Teen's Heart*, p. 249.
24. Gray, "A Big Old Grin," *Stories for a Teen's Heart*, p. 68.

25. Charles Swindoll, *Start Where You Are* (Nashville, TN: Word Publishing, 1999), p. 12.

26. Gray, "Tough Decisions," *Stories for a Teen's Heart*, p. 89.

27. Gray, "The Little Town Is Where . . .," *Stories for the Family's Heart*, p. 95.

28. Gray, "Her Path of Love," *Stories for the Family's Heart*, p. 161.

29. Wayne Rice, "The Flying V," *Hot Illustrations for Youth Talks* (El Cajon, CA: Youth Specialties, 1994), p. 95.

30. Joni Eareckson Tada, "Thoughts Midstream," in Gray, *Stories for the Family's Heart*, p. 280.

31. Gray, "A Cup of Tea," *Stories for the Family's Heart*, p. 126.

32. Gray, "The Ring Bearer," *Stories for the Family's Heart*, p. 131.

33. Rice, "The Glove," *Hot Illustrations for Youth Talks*, p. 103.

34. Gray, "Mistaken Identity," *Stories for the Family's Heart*, p. 82.

35. Gray, "Sparky," *Stories for the Family's Heart*, p. 73.

36. Tony Campolo, "The Storm," in Gray, *Stories for the Family's Heart*, p. 144.

ALSO FROM NEIL ANDERSON
AND DAVE PARK

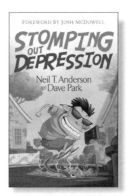

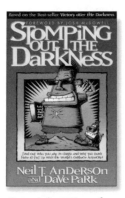
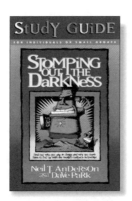
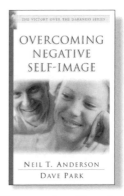